Nothing Left but *Love*

A story about Alzheimer's, Death and a Daughter's Healing Journey

Glenda Rueger Payne

TABLE OF CONTENTS

DEDICATION

This book is lovingly dedicated to my lovely mom, Wanda.
Thank you, Mom, for everything you gave me; even the hard lessons.
To my beautiful, wise sisters who traveled this journey with me.
And to all of you who are currently facing this journey with your
loved ones. May you be uplifted in your dark and lonely hours.

FOREWORD

My Nonno was already receding into the sidelines of Alzheimer's disease when I began to visit my grandparents in their Washington, DC apartment as a young adult. He'd had one or two violent outbursts and often didn't recognize his family. But my Nonna was determined to keep him at home.

Gradually, he no longer ambled to his chair in the living room, no longer joined her for meals at the dining room table. His life became confined to the bedroom, where he was tended by home health aides alongside my Nonna. She told me, when I asked how she could bear it, that it was no longer like the love of a wife for a husband. It had become more like the love of a mother for a child.

My father, a marathon runner driven to Ivy League success, the first in his family to graduate high school, never imagined a life of disability. "Just put a pillow over my head" was the unsentimental way he envisioned calling it quits if he were to become terminally ill.

But when he was diagnosed, a healthy 63 years old, with the worst kind of brain cancer, he wanted every possible day. Despite being unable to speak, write, or walk the way he once had. Even when he could no longer leave his bed. To be read to, to eat the foods he loved, to be blanketed by their four cats – for this once proud and ambitious man, these pleasures of life became enough.

I approached an older couple I'd seen at several Death Cafés about facilitating at a future discussion session. The husband said, yes, they'd like to. But he needed me to know that his wife had

Alzheimer's, so they would have to do this as a team. I assured them that when I asked folks to sit with those they didn't know – a standard Death Café practice – it wouldn't apply to them. "Well actually," the husband said, speaking tenderly to his wife, "every day you're a new person to me, aren't you? And I'm a new person to you. So it does apply to us, too."

These stories, like the one you hold in your hands, are prayer beads to be lingered over, to connect us to the big questions of our times: how to live, how to love, how to die and to forgive. Too often, in contemporary North America, the sick and the old are assigned the status of "other" – no longer included at the heart of family and community life, their value expired. *Nothing Left But Love* is an important antidote to this thoroughly modern malady.

The story of Wanda Deane Baker Rueger and her daughters, told with unsparing honesty by Glenda Rueger Payne, is a story of redemption. This heartfelt book describes a relationship that continued and deepened during Wanda's dying time, and that did not end with her last exhale.

The changes in Wanda's health – the progression of her Alzheimer's and heart disease – were not just the end of something, the "end of life" (which strangely sounds better to the current sensibility than the word "death"). Instead, the unavoidable fact of Wanda's mortality proved to be fertile ground in which healing and reconciliation were birthed.

So few of us grow up with our great aunt dying in the upstairs bedroom anymore. *Nothing Left But Love* brings us to the bedside that's now so often hidden from view. Make no mistake: it's not an easy place to be. As Glenda says, this journey was full of sadness and hardship. We are right there with Wanda as she loses control of her bladder. We're spending sleepless nights with her daughters as they rotate through three unsatisfactory makeshift beds. And we're enfolded in their loving care as they recount moments of sweetness to each other.

Fifteen years after my own father's death, I often wish I'd kept a journal of the 18 months in which I served as one of his two primary caregivers. At the time, it was all so vivid. I thought I would never forget. But the details of those days, and all I might learn from reviewing them once more, have inevitably faded.

The decision Glenda and her sisters made to document their time with their dying mother is a gift to us all. Love Bigly – a phrase inadvertently coined in one of the last birthday cards Glenda wrote her mother – forms the core message of their story. It springs from these pages in the devotion of three daughters to their mother's care. It poignantly underscores the healing that takes place as the author confronts the wounds in her family's past. And it points to a chapter yet unwritten: the ways Wanda will live on.

These days, our self-help obsessed society has turned its fix-it mania on death. A "good death" is the new holy grail. A good death is generally understood as one in which the dying person doesn't suffer, in which they impose as little burden as possible on others.

Wanda's death, presented to us with honesty and courage by Glenda Rueger Payne, offers an alternative understanding of a good death: a death from which we can learn. Glenda turns Wanda's dying and death into the kind of teacher our times so desperately need. This is a story to wonder about, to be troubled by, with the power to touch us and teach us.

Holly J Pruett
Life Cycle Celebrant and
Director of Death Talk Project
HollyPruettCelebrant.com
DeathTalkProject.com

INTRODUCTION

> **"As a well-spent day brings happy sleep,
> so a life well used brings happy death."**
>
> ~ LEONARDO DA VINCI

*B*irth and death are both sacred moments when the world and its constant noise fade away and Love, bigger than you've ever known, declares itself fully. In its Holy Presence, nothing is left but Love. Allowing it is the only requirement.

This story follows my mom, Wanda Deane Baker Rueger's final days as she struggled with both Alzheimer's and congestive heart failure and all of the heartbreaking and miraculous moments my sisters and I shared with her as her caregivers.

In my opinion, these moments are the real guts of life–our reason for being here in the first place. This experience was deeply healing for me. I hope that by sharing our story with you, you will find the courage to heal any family wounds you may still harbor so that you don't miss out on the healing gifts just waiting for you to unwrap them.

Much of what I share in this book comes from a journal we created for Mom. It was originally meant to be a log of our visits since she could no longer remember them. As her disease progressed and reading the journal to her became a moot point, my sisters and I began writing the entries to each other. In the end, it morphed into a remarkable record of her final days.

In her book, "Living at the End of Life," author and Hospice Nurse Karen Whitley Bell, RN describes how one of her patients faced his impending end of life, "I gaze at him looking for signs of fear but see none. Instead, I see a quiet acceptance, wisdom, and a grace rarely found in this time and culture in which we live. Most of us live our lives in haste, in pursuit of goals, in denial: 'I must hurry. I must have more. It will not happen to me'."

I observe that this is the attitude of most people as they move through their busy lives. Often, there is little time allowed to be fully present in body and spirit with our elderly loved ones as they prepare to leave this world. I wrote this book to offer a different perspective.

My journey with my mom's final life stage was full of sadness and hardship. I watched the intelligent woman who was once so full of laughter slowly dissolve away as Alzheimer's, and congestive heart failure ravaged her mind and body. Yet, I felt driven from the core of my being to be by her side until her last breath. I did not know then how my courage held such deep reward.

As difficult as it was to watch her struggle with increasing confusion and delusions from dementia, our story is also full of amazing, emotionally healing moments. If you are dealing with an Alzheimer's diagnosis in your family, I hope this book proves a guide to help you navigate the strange landscape of this bizarre disease.

Explosive anger and abuse filled our household in my early childhood. The subsequent emotional and mental anguish produced by such a volatile environment has been challenging to overcome. The fuel to overcome the challenges came from the laughter and love, which equally filled our home.

I accidentally signed one of the last birthday cards I gave my mom with the phrase, "I love you Bigly." Even though we laughed then at the odd turn of phrase, I later came to believe it was no accident.

As my two sisters and I rallied around our mom during her final days, what I came to feel in my blood, my bones and to the very core of my being is that Loving Bigly comes from something beyond ourselves. It has the power to heal all wounds: if you simply let it.

It is my hope that as you follow our story, you can begin to allow for the possibility that Loving Bigly can heal your life and relationships. Perhaps it will inspire you to make whatever arrangements are necessary to enable you to be 100% focused on your parents as they leave your life for the last time.

Our culture accepts the necessity of this process when our children or spouses die. Often, though, our elderly parents spend their final days alone, cared for only by an underpaid, overwhelmed staff at a care facility. If they are lucky, a dedicated Hospice team whose purpose is devoted entirely to the comfort and support of the dying patient provides the much-needed care. Even so, they cannot provide what loving family members can.

My wish for you is that you, too, can experience how a lifetime of hurt and anger can melt away when you make a choice to Love Bigly. That kind of love is Divinely inspired and moves us beyond the boundaries of our little selves.

It is an energy that is always present though we are usually too wounded, stressed, or busy and distracted to feel it. Some may not even believe it exists. Since it is as real to me as breathing, maybe our story will plant seeds of possibility for you that it does exist. You can find it inside of your own, willing heart.

One important note: When I capitalize words like Love and Presence, it is because I am referring to those qualities emanating from the Divine, the Presence that exists beyond our individual ego selves. Out of respect, I capitalize them just as it is correct to capitalize the words, God and Christ.

I have deliberately made many of my references to my relationship with the Divine in as non-denominational a way as possible. I want you to be able to relate to our story regardless of any religious belief or life philosophy.

My mom raised us in a Christian household, which is evident as you read on. Still, the experiences I share lie outside any particular religious belief structure. In my opinion, connecting through the heart goes beyond such boundaries.

Chapter 1

HOSPICE DAY

*O*ur entry into and exit from this world are the only moments when what is real, true and vibrantly important about life comes into undeniably, crystal-clear focus. And usually, they happen in their own time, which is often not a convenient one. Especially the moment of death. It comes under no one's rule but Its own.

While my sisters and I were moving along in our lives filled with our individual trials and tribulations, my mom Wanda's death forced itself into our lives. My middle sister, Sherry, was still in the throes of deep grief over the loss of her husband to lung cancer just six months prior.

Donna, my eldest sister, had to balance her full-time, demanding career while caregiving her father-in-law as he struggled with Alzheimer's himself. He passed peacefully at home with Donna and her husband Bill as his loving caregivers.

I was still reeling from a forced medical retirement in 2010 due to a rare form of degenerative muscle disease called Mitochondrial Inclusion Body Myositis. It leaves me with so little energy I often need a scooter for most outings. Even doing the dishes can crumple me to the floor. Into this arena, came the reality that my mom's life story was in its final chapter.

Excerpt from my Personal Journal
February 2013

I have to face it. My mom's life is fading away. I feel like I'm watching a candle flame slowly diminish from oxygen deprivation. An apt analogy as the congestive heart failure deprives her brain and body of life-giving oxygen.

Mom's lived in an assisted-living facility for the last five years. She has more room in her little studio apartment than she had at my house. There's a lovely little kitchenette with a small sink, refrigerator, and microwave on the left as you enter her room.

Around the corner you see her bed, dresser, and a mandatory bookshelf for this avid reader filled with her favorite books. She has a comfortable, red, reclining rocking chair and two other rocking chairs for guests. There are three beautiful windows on the east side of her room with a lovely view of the lawn and gardens beyond. Off to the right of her bed, lies her wheelchair accessible bathroom with a large, roll in shower. Soft, neutral, beige tones decorate the walls and floors.

Everything she needs is conveniently close. It's a perfect fit for her. She is content here. I am so glad she likes it. She was no longer safe being home alone while my husband and I were away at work. Due to her dementia, she spends less and less time enjoying the many activities the facility provides.

For the most part, it's an adequate care home. The furniture and decorations reflect a quiet elegance. There are always fresh flowers in the lobby, which opens into the dining room. It has tall windows reaching across the entire West wall from the floor to the cathedral ceiling. The smells of home cooking often waft through the entryway, especially on holidays.

Mom's staff caregivers see her every day and usually only long enough to deliver her medications or remind her of meals. Because she spends most of her time alone in her room, they do not see the increased confusion, inability to dress appropriately, and a growing weakness that leaves her struggling with exhaustion getting from her bed to the bathroom just a few short steps away.

I believe her weaker body signals that Mom is moving to late-stage congestive heart failure. She's so intelligent and convincing in her delusions that they do not recognize that her stories, like having been born with a clubbed foot, are the product of an Alzheimer's demented mind.

I am supposed to take Mom to see her neurologist, but she is so weak that I cannot get her there by myself. I call her doctor and explain what I am witnessing. We discuss that she often can no longer find the right words to express herself, leaving her angry and frustrated. Her intelligence remains clear enough that she knows her brain isn't working, but can't understand why.

He says, "When they lose their words, it's my signal that it is time for Hospice." I call my sisters. It's a weird moment to be discussing the reality of our mom's impending death.

The facility staff gives me the impression that they think I'm premature in my decision to follow her neurologist's advice to declare it's time for Hospice. I know the staff is simply not paying attention and my protective genes go into overdrive.

I contact the local Legacy Hospice team myself because more than a week has passed and I have not heard from them. I explain that I don't believe the facility staff is paying attention. They don't notice the dramatic changes that I see. I visit once or twice a week.

To me, she's in a downward spiral that grows more evident with each visit.

I explain to the hospice intake nurse that it's the congestive heart failure running its course more than the Alzheimer's that has me concerned. She takes a second look at mom's medical information, which substantiates my concerns. We meet the next day and officially enter her into the Hospice program.

Present Day Reflections

Wanda Rueger passed away on June 26, 2013. It seemed a painful death and one difficult to watch. This woman; the one who birthed me, took care of me, argued with me and sometimes hurt me, had become nearly infantile herself.

Though her death was difficult for me to witness, it was time. She was 87 years old, in mental turmoil and constant pain. But still, she was my mom. I miss her even though the mom I had known had been missing for the last few years.

I had to go through my grief and mourning before I was able to confront the memories so vividly rekindled as I read through the pages of our journal. I needed time to heal and rediscover my identity as someone who is no longer a caregiver for her elderly mom, a role I had taken on after my father's death in April of 1996.

February 25, 2013
Glenda's Entry ~ Hospice Begins

Dear Mom,

Today, we entered into the final chapters of your life. Last Fall, we made this journal for you. We write what happens each time we visit. You have Alzheimer's and often don't remember the last time you've seen us. You have the delusion that it has been months, if not years, since we last visited.

At times, you don't always know who we are, though, you have the feeling that you should. Then memory returns and you fall into despair that you didn't know your daughters. It's okay, Mom. We're here with you anyway, and we understand.

We were all here today to meet with the Hospice team, and sign the papers that officially declare we have entered into your end of life journey. I feel sadness and a bit of shock that we are finally here, but also a relief. I'm glad to know your difficulties are coming to an end.

I am relieved to know that our pain and stress, as we watch you disappear, will be over soon, too. And it is helpful knowing that your Hospice team will be here to support us through this difficult journey.

I had a dream the other night that makes more sense now. I glean much of my support and guidance from the natural world. In this dream, the sun was setting as I watched a small, black bear disappear through a waterfall. I remember thinking in the dream as I followed,

"If Bear can do it, so can I!"

Behind the waterfall, I landed on a big conveyor belt. The only choice I had was to hold tight and hang on for the ride to wherever it would carry me. Today, I feel as though I just went through that waterfall with you, Mom.

Your weakness from the congestive heart failure and dementia has been steadily increasing and now it's time to face the inevitable. I'm on board for wherever this end of life journey takes us.

We daughters are now taking turns visiting so that one of us is with you every day. We read to you from this journal to help you understand what's happening and to help you remember who we are.

Our First Entries into Mom's Book
October, 2012

I was born Donna Sue Rueger in Salina, Kansas on October 23, 1950. You were 25 years old and Arvon Rueger, our dad, was almost 29. It's 59 years later, and now my name is Donna Bennington. You have continued to be a woman I look up to, depend on and admire. Just a few years ago, when you and dad lived near my husband and me in Hillsboro, Oregon, I was always leaving my car lights on. Of course, my battery would die. Who would I call to rescue me? You, of course! My loving mother would always come to my aid. I love you!

I was born Sharon Kay Rueger, nicknamed Sherry, on April 21, 1952. We lived in Natoma, Kansas. I am your middle daughter. When I was born, Donna was 18 months and you, Mom, were 26 ½ years old.

When I was a little girl, you made special fairy and butterfly costumes for me and a special cupcake birthday cake that spelled my name. You often made clothes for me and drapes for the windows. You were very creative!

I am now 60 years old. I love you, my very special mom!

I was born Glenda Lynn Rueger on November 7, 1956, in Plainville, KS. You used to call me your little blonde Indian because my olive skin would get darkly tan and my hair was almost white blonde. You were always very intuitive, and I find it interesting that when we all had our DNA tested, I am the only daughter to show a small percentage of Native American blood.

My favorite memory of my early years is how you would play cards with me every night after supper. You always made our birthdays and Christmases such fun, beautiful days!

When we lived in Kansas City, you and I took singing lessons and sang in the church choir together. You were 31 when I was born. I will be 56 next week and am married now. I kept my maiden name and am now called Glenda Rueger Payne.

Today is your 87th birthday. You were born on October 30, 1925. We came to have cake and ice cream with you, and we made you this book. We want you to know how very much loved you are!

February 25, 2013
Sherry's Entry ~ Hospice Day Continues

Your three daughters were all here this afternoon to meet with the Hospice nurse for your assessment. We all stayed with you after your nurse left. Glenda showed you a picture of her cats snuggling together, which made you laugh. Donna read from the book by Lilian Jackson Braun, The Cat Who Robbed a Bank.

You sat in your red lounge chair for a long while until you were ready to lie down and nap. It was just before 3:30 PM.

Present Day Reflections

Mom, as I watched you sitting in your red chair that day, I knew you didn't understand what was happening. We all three surrounded you along with your Hospice care coordinator and intake nurse. At times you disappeared behind the blank, glassy look in your eyes.

Even though I could tell you did not understand what all of the fuss was about, it seemed that you enjoyed being the center of so much focused attention. The Hospice staff told me that a boost in energy is typical after enrollment. They discontinued all of your non-comfort related medications. One of us started visiting you every day instead of only once or twice a week. Your hospice nurses also frequently visited. It may be that all of the attention and medication changes were responsible for your renewed vitality.

At times, I wondered if I had been premature in my insistence that you needed Hospice care, even though the doctor ordered it. It soon became apparent that I had made the right choice. It was a strange, overwhelming, and yet, very precious time.

I will be telling our story, including the unpleasant details. It's important to share the reality of what happened. The miraculous moments are made even more brilliantly clear when contrasted against the darker, painful ones.

Witnessing your body disintegrate, along with the personality I knew as you, was the most frightening and exhausting task I've ever undertaken. It was also, by far, the most miraculous and rewarding. I am grateful for the experience and for having known you as my mom.

The Rueger Women

We gathered at Mom's apartment for her final birthday
celebration on October 30, 2012.
In order: Donna, Mom, Me and Sherry

Chapter 2

THE UNWANTED ONE

> **"...People will hate you, rate you, shake you and break you. But how strong you stand is what makes you."**
>
> ~ AUTHOR UNKNOWN

November 7, 1956, marked the arrival date of the third daughter born to Wanda and Arvon Rueger of Plainville, KS. My oldest sister, Donna, was six and Sherry, my middle sister, was four and a half. Being only 18 months apart, they were very close. They did not welcome this noisy brat of a little sister.

Years later I found out Sherry felt she had lost the dad she worshiped as his attention diverted to me. Donna and I have never spoken of her feelings about my birth. Though I remember some moments of fun and play between us and a fight or two, we didn't get to know each other until after she left for college. I'm assuming she was not very pleased.

Mom, at 31, was not thrilled either. As the wife of the town dentist and a career woman herself, she was frustrated merely being housewife and mother. She had inherited too much of her own mother's resentment against a culture that did not accept women as capable and intelligent enough to have a career beyond their duties of raising a family. She abhorred housework and found it unequal stimulation to her own brilliant, scientific mind.

She was so looking forward to getting her life and freedom back when Sherry was old enough to attend Kindergarten that fall. But while she was busy making her plans, I happened. I was a total surprise given that they had difficulty conceiving the first time and felt lucky to have two beautiful daughters. My parents never expected a third child. Suddenly, Mom was looking at four more years of being housebound with another, rather colicky, baby girl.

I remember very clearly being little enough that I am sitting in the grocery cart basket as Mom shops. I'm too young to have many words yet. As I watch her grumpily sorting through the packages of meat, I know that she is not happy and that I must not do anything to call attention to myself. She seems angry a lot of the time.

When I am three, we are in the kitchen. Mom is in that grumpy mood again and very focused on the nasty job of oven cleaning as I sit on the floor beside her. All I know is that I am bored and I want her to play with me. So I reach out and give her a pat on her bottom. She ignores me. I laugh and pat her again. She still ignores me. So I pat her yet again, a little harder and laughing more loudly. Without a word, she grabs me and spanks me hard and puts me to bed. I'm left alone, hurt, crying and not understanding why my very presence seems to make my mom so angry.

I already felt unwanted and unwelcome by mom's behavior. My two big sisters contributed to my feelings by ganging up and teasing me relentlessly. I continued to feel unwelcome throughout my childhood. I remember thinking several times, "if you did not want me, why did you have me?" I frequently wished I had never been born.

My dad often displayed an unpredictable, violent temper. I remember being around three or four. Mom was gone. I loved hearing my Dad's great stories. He also enjoyed making us laugh. So we were snuggled in his bed, and he was telling me funny stories.

He heard Mom come home and asked me if I wanted to stay there or return to my room. I said I would stay there, thinking that they would come and be with me soon. But as time moved on, I became bored. I remembered he said that if I made the decision to stay there, I could not change my mind and go to my room. But that did not make any sense to me so off I went to my bed and sleep.

Suddenly I was awakened by Dad demanding I roll over so he can beat me with a ruler because I went to bed instead of staying in his room. I remember Donna being mad at me for crying loudly enough to wake her up. Sherry told her I was crying because Dad woke me up to beat me.

Dad's head games were weird enough to an adult mind but wholly inexplicable to a young child. My sisters didn't understand it any more than I did. Dad used to tease us a lot. But, his teasing face and his angry face were so similar that we never knew if the moment would end with a tickle or the belt.

When I was seven, Dad sold his dental practice and moved the family to Kansas City, MO. He had slipped a disc in his back on the night I was born and was in constant pain. He never fully healed from that injury. His back pain made it impossible for him to continue in private practice. That could have been part of the underlying fuel for his weird, unpredictable moments of rage.

I found out in my adult years that Dad didn't know he was adopted until entering the military during WWII. His birth certificate revealed that he'd been born on December 3, 1921. His parents had always celebrated his birthday on his adoption day in April 1922.

Dad suddenly realized he was four months older. That realization filled him with a sense of rejection and unresolved anger at his birth mom for abandoning him and his adopted parents for having lied to him his entire life.

What I respected about my dad is that he was truly brilliant. Had the tools for personal growth and emotional healing been as available to him in his time as they are to us now, he might have found enough healing and self-esteem to pursue his interests in Kirlian photography as a hobby. Kirlian photography is a technique that captures the electrical coronal discharges given off by living things. Dad expressed his natural gifts by pursuing photography as a hobby and exploring various life philosophies.

Instead of pursuing his passion as a career, he slogged through life in a professional role influenced more by his parents than by personal choice. He once told me he gave up his dreams for a career that offered him the financial security to provide for his family and make his parents proud.

In my teen years, Dad often told me how being a dentist had made him come to hate people. He had said in one of our heart to heart talks that he didn't believe in happiness. Sadly, I do not know if he passed without ever really knowing what true happiness is.

Reconciling my compassion for his unhappiness with my anger at the man who had made up reasons beyond my comprehension for punishing me felt insurmountable at times. In my early thirties, I began to have terrifying flashbacks. I realized that some of the spankings had very confusing elements resulting in feelings of betrayal and sexual molestation, even though I can't know that was his intent.

I remember him telling me once I needed a spanking for something I had no recollection of doing, let alone understanding why I deserved punishment. He took me into his bedroom, turned me over his knee and pulled down my panties.

There I am straddled over his lap expecting pain. When suddenly I realize that what he is doing feels good. He's gently caressing me between my legs.

I think to myself, "Wow, this isn't so bad. Maybe he won't hurt me after all!"

Just then he delivers several hard slaps to my naked butt. I'm shocked! My feelings hurt even more from the betrayal of pleasure turned into sharp, stinging pain. There were other instances. I think they finally stopped when I was around four.

My dad's life was full of emotional and physical pain, which he liberally shared with us. Finally, the back pain from the slipped disc made it impossible for him to continue as a private dentist. He sold his practice to become a professor at the Dental School of the University of Missouri at Kansas City.

After our move, big city schools proved even more challenging for me. As the youngest, littlest class member I was shy and withdrawn. I felt I didn't understand anything I was supposed to be able to, especially if the subject was math.

In my memory, Sherry was always a brilliant, straight A student, though she disagrees with me on that point now. Donna was an avid reader who seemed to thrive socially in the academic environment, which totally baffled me. I just felt like I was the stupid one in the family.

When I was nine, my life changed forever. I couldn't fight my sadness anymore and couldn't face another day of feeling hopeless. I started popping aspirin pills into my mouth one after the other.

It was a pivotal moment that ushered in my life as a mystic because I clearly heard what I believe to be my Guardian Angel saying, "Glenda, stop! There is so much more to come." And so I did stop. And for the first time in my life I felt that I was not alone.

From that moment, even through the pain and sadness of feeling

I didn't belong and wasn't wanted, I became aware of the underlying presence of Love. I felt it in moments when I ran barefoot through the wilderness creek across the street from my house. I felt it when I took Winter walks alone in our backyard under the crystal, clear glistening skies. I felt it in the whispering winds and the rustling leaves. And I felt it when I secretly stole my way into the empty sanctuary of the Methodist Church next to my Grandparent's house in Pratt, KS.

I remember standing in the moonlight hearing soft whispers in the trees saying, "Glenda, remember who you are!" It would be years before I understood what they meant. But those whispers fueled me through the dark times when I wanted to give up.

Throughout my early years, in spite of all the sadness and pain, there were also moments of happiness and wonder. When I was little, Dad would show me magic tricks and make me giggle and laugh as I sat in his lap while Mom prepared dinner. Then she would play cards with me each evening as we relaxed with TV.

Though Donna and Sherry were often mean in their relentless teasing, we also had great fun playing together. They took turns pushing me off of their feet to launch me into the air. We pretended I could fly all the way back home. Fortunately, they didn't launch me far. Imagining I could fly was thrilling!

Mom and Dad taught us all to enjoy and appreciate nature through woodland outings, picnics by the lake and family vacations in Grandmother and Granddaddy's Mill Creek cabin. We spent summers with friends at the Lake of the Ozarks. The Garland family who owned the vacation home had a son and three daughters. We girls were all best friends.

Those fun times helped me through the angry years when Dad was addicted to Darvon due to the constant back pain. In those times, he disappeared into a drug induced stupor. Mom had gone back to work as a medical technologist when we moved and seemed withdrawn from me when she was home.

Now I can understand that disappearing into TV land every night was her coping skill. I remember needing help with my homework. Her only response to my questions was, "How can I watch TV if I have to help you with your homework!" At the time, I just continued to feel how much of an intrusion I seemed to be in her life.

Still, we survived. I survived. As I grew, we came to know each other as people rather than just family members. My sisters morphed from mean, big sisters to women I admire, respect and feel very lucky to now call my best friends. I believe the many fun, laughter filled moments we all shared together helped us grow close in spite of the icky, angry times. Sharing laughter was, and still is, how we express caring for each other.

As I grew, my parents and I did finally find our way to genuine friendship. For that, I am incredibly grateful. It is a wonder to begin to see our family members as people rather than locking them into whatever family role we've assigned to them in our minds.

When Donna and Sherry both left to pursue their lives, Mom and I grew closer. She never did talk much about her life and childhood. Grandmother was a strict, teetotaling Methodist not prone to nurturing and warm fuzzies. Mom once said, without giving any details, "I can never forgive my mom for what she did to me."

As my journey continued, I strove to find the meaning in life and my purpose for being here. Once I graduated from the left-brained focus of the academic system, I came to understand and appreciate that I am intelligent. I just didn't learn the way the traditional school system taught.

I launched into my a self-study program of psychology,

comparative religion, and various philosophers. College courses were easier for me to navigate. I rounded out my self-studies with courses in Philosophy, Communications and English Literature at UMKC.

I fought hard to explore my intrinsic value and garner better self-esteem. Reading the book, "I'm Okay, You're Okay," by Thomas A. Harris, MD, first published in 1969, finally freed me from feeling I didn't even have the right to breathe. The Angels continued to uplift me in dreams and whispers.

I came to know and love my dad for his bright intellect, his witty sense of humor, and his willingness to always laugh at himself. He was a talented photographer who gave me my first camera when I was only four.

Every Saturday was photography day. We were either taking pictures, developing them in the darkroom or exploring as many camera stores as we could find. We once drove all the way from Kansas City to Chicago and back in one day just to visit a leading camera equipment store.

As a young adult, our family dinners were either filled with deep philosophical discussions or were scenes of raucous laughter as Dad would turn the various experiences of his day into entertaining stories.

Dad was nearly deaf. He would explain his very bizarre interpretations of what he thought his students had said. One afternoon, a young woman entered the elevator with him. He heard, "Hi ya Sweetie!" He politely acknowledged her with an embarrassed nod of his head. When repeating her words for the third time, she finally shouted, "PUSH FIVE, PLEASE!"

He also had no sense of direction. He shared how he'd get lost trying to find his way to a specialty store across the state line. He kept turning onto back streets ending in Kansas cornfields. He taught us that laughing at ourselves is a great coping skill!

My dad and I shared a sense of awe at the mystical side of life. When I was in sixth grade, he suffered a series of severe heart attacks. In those days, they didn't do bypass surgery, and exercise of a weak heart was thought to be a bad thing. He spent weeks in the hospital.

When he got home, he shared something with me that had left him in awe. He was awakened in the middle of the night by a strong Presence in the room. He heard the words, "Do not fear for your family. No matter what happens to you, they will always be taken care of."

Then the Presence visited two other occupants of the four-bed hospital ward. The next day the hospital Chaplain, whom Dad had never before spoken to, came and prayed with him and then the other two whom the Presence had also visited. Dad told me the story shortly after his release. He said he felt I was the only one who would understand.

Perhaps my ability to tune into the frequency and vibration of a spiritual Presence, a being of such unconditional, boundless Love, was born during those dark and lonely days of my childhood.

Somehow, the power of Love and the bonds we formed helped our family find healing and forgiveness in spite of the chaotic, awful times. We chose loving and compassion over anger, resentment and hate.

As I write this at the age of 58, I am grateful that I am passionately driven to heal myself and to share my healing stories. I hope that my story might inspire you to find courage enough to do your emotional healing work, too.

I discovered that there is always Love available to us whenever we are ready to accept it. Love with a capital L is way beyond our sense of romantic or even family love. Big Love is much deeper than that. The path to it lies within.

Perhaps it was no mistake that I once signed Mom's birthday card with the words, "I love you bigly!" By the Grace of this experience, I now understand what Loving Bigly does for the soul. Since that was one of the last birthday cards I ever gave her, my soul probably knew it then, too.

Chapter 3

BECOMING MOM'S MOM

"Parenthood... It's about guiding the next generation, and forgiving the last."

~PETER KRAUSE

The mom I most remember had amazing alabaster skin, beautiful freckles, and strawberry blonde hair from our Celtic heritage. She could be very cheerful and bubbly and loved dancing, though her attempts at teaching me the Jitterbug failed miserably.

She stood on a sturdy, 5'5" frame and always had the most beautiful, long fingernails. Mine have never been that strong. She enjoyed her career in medical technology, and I know, in spite of everything, that she loved her family very much.

Grandmother was always very strict. Yet, she married a very compassionate, loving man. I didn't find out until we were studying our genealogy recently that Granddaddy's parents were Quakers.

Granddaddy's quiet and gentle ways might have balanced Grandmother's harsh parental style. As things went in those days, the rearing of children was Grandmother's domain. She ruled mom with an iron will leaving her with a smoldering anger that never went away.

Mom was also very caring and compassionate at times in spite of the underlying tinge of anger. Expressing her feelings was never easy for her. Sometime in my 21st year, we finally learned how to talk about our feelings with each other. That was an important part of healing between us. Though, the seeds for healing were planted when I was ten.

Shortly after my suicide attempt at the age of nine, which I never disclosed to her, the school finally alerted my parents to the fact that I had missed a total of one month of schooling.

I had been skipping either a Wednesday or Thursday each week. Skipping school started the day my dad had the first of his heart attacks. Donna flipped on my bedroom light one morning fifteen minutes before my usual wake up time with the words, "You have to get up now. Mom took Dad to the hospital. They think he had a heart attack." Then she and Sherry promptly left for school.

I was totally stunned by that news and left completely alone in our big house. It never felt so empty as in that moment. I was too emotionally overwhelmed to face another day of feeling stupid at school with a teacher who seemed to delight in humiliating me. I just stayed home. I began to repeat that pattern on a weekly basis.

When it was time for my sisters to arrive home from their school days, always earlier than my scheduled arrival time, I quietly walked into the woods across the street and stayed hidden until my regular time.

As my school struggles finally became evident to my parents they decided to have me tested. The results were that I was brilliant, but had what they described as a "mental block." I just couldn't process math or understand why. Therefore, I was unable to ask questions; a fact which seemed to infuriate my teacher.

One of the questions on the assessment sheet was,

"What is a home?"

When asked, I just sat in stunned, embarrassed silence for a few minutes before finally saying in meek voice,

"I don't know. It's just a place where you live."

In his follow-up report to my parents, the psychologist said to Mom, "Do you know that your daughter doesn't know what a home is?" Donna told me that mom felt shocked by that news.

Perhaps it was the first time mom realized how absent she'd been in my life after our move. She became much kinder and more understanding to me then. She changed to part time hours so that she could see me onto the school bus each morning and was home when I got back from school. Finally, I felt a much more welcome part of her life.

We went to therapy sessions together. I remember the day our therapist tried to get her to confront her anger with Grandmother. He wanted her to imagine her mom in an empty chair and express her feelings to her. Mom's stubborn streak kicked in, and she clamped up adamantly refusing.

She said, "That's stupid!"

The therapist kept at her, and she kept refusing. I felt her humiliating embarrassment as keenly as if it were my own. The feeling was so intense that I just wanted to cry for her. I believe my desire to fiercely protect my mom arrived in that moment.

Sadly, many people never muster the courage to face their Shadow Selves, as often happens in healing work. That was certainly true for my mom. She made the decision that we didn't need any further help and discontinued the sessions.

Still, it was enough that we began to lay the foundation for a stronger bond with each other. As the years wound on we never lost it again.

January 4, 2013
Glenda's Entry

When I arrived at 1:30 PM you were sitting in your power chair dubbed, "your Royal Chariot." Apparently, you'd been there since lunch. Your oxygen line was tangled up and wrapped around your wheelchair and your head. You had probably been sitting there like that unable to move for about a half hour.

I pulled your emergency cord for a caregiver to come and help me untangle you. After getting you all extricated and everything put to rights, you were very tired. You started talking about how you were ready to just, "not wake up." Then you remembered that I called you this AM just to say, "good morning!" We sure love you!

January 8, 2013
Glenda's Entry

You had just come back from lunch when I arrived a little after 1 PM. I helped you transfer your oxygen from the portable tank to the room concentrator so you could get to the bathroom more easily with your walker rather than driving in on your Royal Chariot.

I brought your scrapbooks to you from Pratt and Kansas City. There are three of them: your Pratt High School graduation, your early college and birthday book, and your college graduation book.

We started looking through the scrapbooks, but you quickly fell asleep. Your massage therapist came just after your nap. You hadn't thought anyone had visited you for awhile. Apparently, you mentioned that to your table mate at lunch. She gave me quite the earful about neglecting you. I told her about this log of our visits.

We try to help you remember that you are very much loved and not forgotten. The last time I was here, you slept through much of my visit. So I don't blame you for not remembering that I was here. I am glad to see you are resting well right now. See you soon. Love you very much.

January 10, 2013
Glenda's Entry

Today is a rough day for you. You are not feeling well, but not able to tell me what's wrong. Your only comment is, "Nothing feels right." Your left arm is trembling, but your grip is fine. The nurses came to check, but your vitals appear normal. They are going to check you for a bladder infection.

Whatever the reason, it is clear that you are physically not feeling OK. In fact, you look pretty miserable. You are complaining of pain in your arms and shoulders though you can't describe how it feels. You just keep saying, "I don't know how I feel."

I'm sorry, Mom. I don't know how to make you feel better. According to the Hospice nurses, phantom pains are part of the Alzheimer's experience.

January 18, 2013
Glenda's Entry

I came by in the afternoon. You had a bad episode before I arrived of confusion and disorientation. The staff medical aid said that you were doing something with your shoes. You kept trying to stuff them into the kitchen drawers, etc. She said it was clear that you did not know what you were doing.

Sherry came by earlier this week. She arrived in the evening.

You were sitting in your Royal Chariot completely blanked out. She helped you switch oxygen and get into your jammies.

Today, you and I spoke on the phone before I got here. You sounded very chipper at 7:30 AM. You were heading to breakfast.

By the time, I arrived you were sound asleep. You woke up enough to go to the bathroom but nearly fell asleep on the toilet. I helped you back into your bed. You complained of hip pain, so I rubbed pain gel into your hip. Your oxygen tube was off and tucked by your feet, so I untangled it and put it back on. You fell asleep before I could get you dressed again.

You woke up long enough to say that your hip was hurting, then you went right back to sleep. We are all worried about you. A little later, you awoke again, got dressed and went right back to bed still complaining about the pain. You mumbled that it felt like something had dropped on your left hip. All I could do was reapply the pain gel.

January 24, 2013
Sherry's Entry

Glenda and I came to visit you today and to meet with your Medicaid caseworker. He was doing an assessment to see if you need an increased level of care to ensure your safety. The concern is that you get confused about which hallway leads to the dining room and have been heading toward the outside door by mistake.

Once, you went outside at night in the rain. So we talked about ways to alert the staff if you leave your room. The facility manager said that there are alarms set on the outside doors, but they only work at night. When you got out, it must have been before activation time.

When we arrived, you were on your way to lunch but headed down the wrong hallway to the outside door again. Your staff had already brought your tray to your room, but you didn't realize that.

It took a bit of effort to make you understand that your food was in your room, so you didn't need to get to the dining room.

Back in your room, you ate your lunch while we talked with your caseworker. I told you what we were discussing with him. After you had eaten, you were very sleepy, so you got back into bed for a nap. The three of us left to talk to the facility manager.

When we came back you had fallen asleep, but woke up. You sat up but had a hard time keeping your eyes open. You were able to talk with us a little, but mostly you needed to lie down with your eyes closed. We left you sleeping.

February 1, 2013
Sherry's Entry

Hi Mom, It's Sherry. I came to visit at 3:40 PM. When I got here, you were lying on your bed with no bedding except a pillow case. So I put clean sheets and a pillowcase on your bed for you while you sat in the rocking chair. I also helped you with your oxygen.

I noticed that one of your bathroom drawers was sitting empty by your bed while the contents were on your bathroom floor. So I reorganized your bathroom supplies in the drawer and put the drawer away. I put your clean clothes and towels away, too. I had found them neatly folded sitting on your closet floor.

I can't stay for an extended visit because this is Imbolc fire pit night at Glenda's. I will be burning some of the flowers from Chuck's memorial service that I had saved for this purpose. My husband, Chuck, passed away six months ago.

February 3, 2013
Glenda's Entry

10:10 AM. When I got here, you were in the bathroom still wearing your night shirt and very tired. I'm not sure if you made it to breakfast. You fell asleep at 10:20. I sat in the red chair, sent you some healing Reiki energy and rested beside you until it was time for me to leave.

February 11, 2013
Glenda's Entry

I arrived just as you were getting a Healing Touch massage. You were in your red chair looking pretty bright eyed. You dozed just a little. I shaved your chin as your crone hairs were pretty long. For some reason, your underwear drawer was empty on your bed, and your undies were stuffed in the space where your drawer should have been. I replaced the drawer and reloaded it.

The facility had a Mardi Gras parade today. The colorfully dressed participants came to your door bearing masks, blowing horns and handing out gold coins for good wishes and prosperity. It was fun to see you laughing and smiling!

February 14, 2013
Donna's Entry

Happy Valentine's Day! Today, I told you about my long-time co-worker and colleague who passed away this morning. We had known each other and worked together for more than thirty years.

She's the one who took the quilt squares your mother had created while she was still alive and made them into the quilt that's now on your bed. After we had talked, I read some more from *The Cat Who Robbed a Bank*. Then I helped you get ready and walked you down to supper.

Sherry's Entry
Same Day

I told you about my day seeing a movie, Les Miserables, with Glenda and one of her close friends. We went to coffee afterward and stayed there too long. We ended up driving home in rush hour traffic.

It took us 1.5 hours to travel the 28 miles to McMinnville from Tigard; a trip that is usually less than an hour. We ate supper at the Thai restaurant with Glenda's husband, Michael, and then I came here to see you. I arrived just after 8 PM, and you were in your jammies, but still awake.

February 18, 2013
Glenda's Entry

I came by in the afternoon. You were awake and pretty chipper. Woohoo! We talked again about how much you want a wrist watch with big numbers. I will look for one, but as I watch your brain disease progression, I'm not sure if you will be able to read and understand it. Telling time is getting difficult for you.

Donna came by, too. After I had left, she read to you from *The Cat Who Robbed a Bank*. She walked you down to supper on her way home.

February 23, 2013
Glenda's entry

I arrived at 12:45 PM. You were just finishing your noon meal in the dining room. We walked to your room together. I discovered that your oxygen was off the tube and disconnected. I pulled your emergency cord for a caregiver. When she came in, she said that they were aware and the med aids were searching for a connector.

Three hours later, after no one showed up, I called again. The new med aid said that the afternoon shift didn't know anything about it. I called the medical supply company myself and resolved the situation.

I was very unhappy that you had been without oxygen for three hours. I spoke to the facility manager to make sure this never happened again. We created a protocol indicating who to call immediately if there is a problem with your oxygen. We listed where we keep your extra supplies. I posted the proper procedures list to your wall.

The facility has had difficulty with you cutting your oxygen tubing into millions of itty-bitty pieces, so they had to take all of the scissors out of your room. Methinks you are protesting your being tethered to an oxygen tube 24/7.

After all of that was handled, you mostly rested and said very little. We did have a discussion about how tired you are. I told you that the staff will deliver your meals to your room. Then you decided you wanted to go to supper anyway. I helped you get ready and walked you to the dining room on my way out.

February 25, 2013
Sherry's Entry

It's Saturday. Glenda and I visited with you most of the day. You had some severe pain in your right thigh, but it subsided with pain meds. The Hospice nurse came around 3:30 PM and all of your vitals were good, with 99% oxygen saturation.

Glenda went home around 6 PM. I visited until around 8:30 and read to you from the book, *Proof of Heaven, A Neurosurgeon's Journey into the Afterlife* by Eben Alexander, MD, which you seemed to enjoy. You wanted me to continue reading. Your eyes were closed, but you were listening.

You fell asleep around 7:45 PM, but woke again at 8:20 because you coughed. You said, "I think it's time to go to bed," and closed your eyes. You opened them again to ask the time then turned over and went back to sleep. When I left, you were still quietly resting.

March 5, 2013
Glenda's Entry

I arrived at 1:36 PM. I brought your supplies of TP, paper towels, lotion, lozenges, mouthwash and body soap. Yesterday, you had such a splendid day. But today, you've been hallucinating that construction workers are in your room.

Apparently, you tried to leave your apartment with just your bathrobe on, which is small enough on you that it won't properly close. I think I'll take this robe home with me when I leave as they tell me you are obsessed with it.

We asked the facility to make sure you have your oxygen on every time they come in your room. The staff checked on you hourly and usually found you'd taken it off. At least, you have not found any more pairs of scissors to cut the tube into a million little pieces. I think you're taking the oxygen hose off because your nose is running so much you blow it often. Then you forget to put it back on. Your O^2 saturation level was at 92% with it off.

You are presently dozing in your red chair. Your hands and feet are extremely cold. I put socks on your feet and covered you with the blue blanket. That helped. You look a bit pale to me today. You doze for a few minutes, squirm around and then doze again.

Since I've been here, you have not had any hallucinations. You woke up, and we've been talking about memories of Robin, Sherry's son who drowned when he was two. It was a hard loss for us all, but especially her.

We then joked about being a family of such cat lovers that your three daughters were much better at giving you grand kittens rather than grandchildren. Since I was never able to have children, Donna was left to pass on the Rueger genes to her only son who has a son of his own (and now a daughter, too!). They live too far away to visit often. You said that you didn't miss having any grandchildren. You thought you might have enjoyed them, but it hadn't worked out that way.

I mentioned that you always had been able not to stress about what you couldn't control. Then you said, "Last week or the week before they had to turn the heater on high because the cats got cold." I smiled a little at that. You have no cats in your room with you.

You didn't eat much of your supper-not even dessert—just too worn out. We put on your penguin PJs, brushed your hair and made a final trip to the bathroom for your evening ablutions. You were quiet and asleep by 6:30 PM and still sleeping when I left at 7 PM.

March 10, 2013
Donna's Entry

I arrived around 12:45 PM and came to your room only to discover you must be eating in the dining room. I put away the things I brought with me and was catching up on your journal notes when you returned from lunch. You were not wearing a bra, and you didn't have your oxygen with you. I don't think your aid anticipated that you were eating lunch in the dining room. You have taken to eating most of your meals in your room.

After a potty break, you napped for awhile. I brought my portable boombox from home and played one of your CDs for you. An hour later, you decided you wanted to dress so you changed into a bra, and the purple outfit Sherry got out for you yesterday.

I read the first two chapters of Nora Roberts' book, *Blithe Images*, one of her early romances. Your med aid came in once, but forgot to take your vitals after I told her about your going down to lunch without your oxygen and no bra.

She discovered that your portable oxygen bottle was empty. As she was taking care of that, she was called away to attend another resident, which is why she didn't get a chance to take your vitals.

Later, when your aid came in to take your supper order, you looked so tired I thought it best we eat in your room. You are now listening to classical music and dozing in your chair. Supper arrived after your nap. Alas, it was not what you ordered, about which you are not too thrilled. You did eat your corn chowder, and I'm sure the cherry pie was a big hit.

We've been playing some *Best of the Big Band Sounds, Vol. 4* of *Entertainers of WWII* from the *Reader's Digest* compilation series. You grew tired of the music, so I turned it off and read a little more from *Blithe Images*. You are getting ready for bed, and I will be leaving shortly after putting your dentures to soak.

March 13, 2013
Sherry's Entry

When I arrived at 2PM, you were up, dressed and turning the dial on your fan for cooler air. I opened the windows since it was so nice out. Spring is blooming!

You went to the bathroom and then sat in your red chair. I sat here quietly writing this while you dozed. At 2:30 I helped you to the bathroom again and then you rested in bed. I told you the story of the Diana Gabaldon books about Jamie and Claire Fraser and the time travel between cultures.

We filed a couple of your fingernails, and then you rested again. After your rest, I read to you from *A Breath of Snow and Ashes* by Diana Gabaldon until 4:30. We had supper in your room, and your caregiver told me that you had eaten all of your meals in your room that day.

Though you need to rest often, you nevertheless are having a lucid day and are enjoying the story. Your only confusion today was thinking you needed to put your pajama bottoms on when you had already changed. But you understood when I showed you that you were already wearing pajamas. You even remembered to put your O_2 on after changing into your pajama top.

You were tired though and didn't eat much of your supper. At 6:30, I helped you get your dentures soaking and rinse your mouth with Biotene®. You said, "It's definitely time for bed." I stayed long enough to call Glenda, write this up and left at 7:10 PM.

March 14, 2013
Glenda's Entry

I arrived at 12:15 PM. You were asleep. You opened your eyes briefly to wave at me, and then went right back to sleep. Your notes indicate that you had a quiet morning. Your breakfast tray is still here.

You had a shower earlier, which could be why you're sleeping so much. Your healing touch massage therapist Debbie came at 1:30. That put you into an even deeper sleep.

3 PM – You're still resting quietly. I just found out from the caregiver that they have an outbreak of Norovirus. We all have to wear masks, and are confined to eating all meals in your room. The dining room is closed and they canceled all group activities for 36 hours. Glad you are not showing any symptoms of it so far!

You seem to be having difficulty recognizing objects today. I had to show you the soap bottle so you could wash your hands. Other than that, you are pretty lucid when awake.

You were fatigued after eating supper. We changed you into your nightie, washed your face and put your dentures to soak. Then you immediately went to bed. You looked as tired as if you had walked a mile. You were asleep by the time I left at 6:15.

March 15, 2013
Glenda's Entry

I arrived at 12:50 PM to see that you had eaten all of your lunch. You again have such little energy. I spoke to your Hospice nurse who visited you at 10 AM. She said that you slept deeply through her entire visit.

When I arrived, you were still sitting in front of your tray table. I cleared away your lunch dishes and helped you to the bathroom, then to bed. You rested until 3 PM when you moved to the red chair. You were hungry enough to snack on some yogurt, which you enjoyed. After that, you dozed until 4:44.

Then you got mad. You weren't hungry because you had just eaten the yogurt, but were restless, worn out and told me that you were sick of feeling that way. You mentioned Dad about three times today.

Then you were trying to tell me a story about a caregiver having something on her back, and others were joining in. Something I had said sparked this conversation. You were having trouble finding your words. I never did understand what you were trying to say. I think you weren't tracking well, so the story kept morphing into other things.

You continued to get more agitated and uncomfortable. I called your Hospice nurse and asked if some medication might help. She agreed it would and said she would call the staff med aid.

A Hospice volunteer delivered a bedside commode for you earlier this afternoon. That created even more agitation. I finally figured out that you were worried about being billed for new equipment. I explained that your insurance paid 100% of the costs so you wouldn't be getting a bill. Your staff caregiver brought you some Lorazepam at 5 PM.

You started severely hallucinating around 6 PM or so. You got even more agitated and angry because you didn't understand what was happening. You didn't know where you were or how long you'd be there.

It seemed like you thought you were in the hospital. You started saying that, "they," (I think you meant the doctors or the hospital people) started in at noon putting some kind of screw in your neck. You were worried that your head would fall off.

Then you started saying something was wrong with your legs, and that they wouldn't work. I touched them and asked if you could wiggle your toes. As you could feel my touch and move them, it calmed you a little.

Then you became angry because you felt no one was telling you what was going on. I think it's because I left your room to talk to the Hospice nurse about a possible reaction to the Lorazepam. I told you that we were talking about your meds as they seemed to be making you more uncomfortable, but it didn't resolve your agitation.

So, I sat on the bed with you and told you that you had heart failure and a brain disease and that your body was failing. I explained that the doctors, nurses and everyone here was doing everything they could to make you comfortable.

Your reply was, "Well, it's not working!"

I said, "I know." I told you this reminds me of the times you made me milk toast when I was sick and feeling miserable. You couldn't make my sickness go away, but you could give me some comfort.

I said, "We're just trying to make you milk toast."

Chapter 4

WHERE YOU GO,
I CANNOT FOLLOW

> ## "One thing you've taught me is the importance of strength even when fear is staring you in the face."
>
> ### ~ G. R. Payne

March 16, 2013
Glenda's Entry

*Y*ou received your Haldol dose at 8:30 PM. Then you did sleep, but you sat bolt upright at 8:45 still feeling very restless. Perhaps you are just uncomfortable from being in one position too long. You got yourself all skiddywampus in the bed. I thought you were going to agitate yourself right onto the floor.

Your caregiver came in then and helped me straighten you out. We rolled you over to your other side, and I put a pillow behind your back for extra support. That seemed to calm you, and you went to sleep until your supper arrived.

After eating, I helped you transfer from your red chair back to bed. You pointed to the floor by the bed and said,

"Is Sherry sleeping there?"

Of course, Sherry is not here with us now. (Interesting to note that where she was pointing did, in fact, become one of our sleeping stations during the last days of her life.)

You said, "I don't want to leave you girls, but I'm ready to leave everything else." We then talked about it being okay with your daughters for you to go. I told you that you did a great job with us and that we would be fine. I said, "You've been a really good mom to us."

We talked about how when Grandmother and Uncle Wayne passed, they both came to say goodbye to me. I told you that I believe you will be able to visit us, too.

At 9:15 PM you're sleeping. I'm going to wait until 10 PM before I think about going home. You have your sleeping pill on board along with your pain meds, so I am more confident that you will sleep through the night now. It took two caregivers to help you to your bedside commode. It is getting hard for you to navigate turns and you are much weaker now.

Oops – I was headed out the door when you woke up coughing and spitting. It took two tries for you to cough everything out. Then we had to wash your chin so I'm still here at 10:40 PM. I'll wait a few minutes to be sure you really are settled down for the night.

March 17, 2013
Sherry's Entry

You were resting on your bed but opened your eyes when I came in at 2:05 PM. I gave you a hug and then showed you that I had brought you two new T-shirts and another pair of jammy bottoms.

I saw that your laundry had been washed, but was put away in strange places. I reorganized and hung up your clothes including all of your jammies since you now have a commode blocking access to your chest of drawers.

You seemed a bit out of sorts so I started reading to you again from the Proof of Heaven book. I read the parts where he describes the other realms he visits. You asked if I was ready to go there.

I replied, "It would sure be interesting."

I then asked if you were and you said, "Not really."

Being read to seems to calm you down but then you get irritated again when you can't figure out how to do something, like hanging up the towel in the bathroom or when you can't find your lozenges.

They brought you creamy chicken dinner and chicken soup for supper with Jello for dessert. You ate half of the chicken, which you said was delicious. You ate all of your dessert and drank your chocolate milk. You said that even though dinner tasted good, you were too full to eat all of it. After supper, I read more of Proof of Heaven to you.

6:40 PM. After a bathroom trip and necessary clean up, we put your dentures to soak and rinsed out your mouth with Biotene®. I helped you into your white nightie with the blue flowers and you climbed into bed.

I noticed that you had used the commode sometime before my arrival, though you've made it all the way into the bathroom during my visit. Before you laid down in bed, you gestured for me to sit down beside you.

You gave me a big hug. I said, "I love you," to which you replied, "and I love you. It's a good thing we love each other."

I said, "Yes, it sure is!" as we exchanged big smiles.

By 7:00 PM you seemed ready to sleep. You rested for a bit, but by 7:15 you were awake. It may be that I made too much noise doing my dishes. Anyway, you woke up annoyed by the oxygen tube and the sheets and blankets. We straightened them out. You laid back down at 7:25, but were still a bit antsy. I read to you some more.

You kept fidgeting with the sheet and blanket. At one point, you said you couldn't figure it out. You also started to take your nightgown off. When I asked why, you asked if it was what you were sleeping in tonight. I said, "Yes, those are the nightie and sheets you are sleeping in tonight."

I decided maybe the story I was reading to you (from the Diana Gabaldon book) was confusing. So I said, "I think I'll stop reading now," and you agreed. You laid down then under the sheet and said goodnight. I took a few minutes to write this and left at 8:30 PM.

March 18, 2013
Sherry's Entry

When I arrived just before 2 PM you were sleeping soundly. The staff chart notes indicate that you had breakfast and lunch in the dining room with escorts to and from your room. You were wearing the dark pink T-shirt with a bra and your beige pants. You woke up at 2:30 PM and went to the bathroom. You then changed into your black velor pants and purple top.

You sat in your antique rocker and rested your eyes occasionally rocking. I put on the CD of the Relax and Unwind with the Classics, another of your favorite Reader's Digest compilations. The music was indeed relaxing and soothing – very beautiful.

I sat next to you in the yellow rocker and wrote these notes, then read quietly to myself while you rested and listened. I put pillows behind your head and back to make it more comfortable for you.

You did have your O^2 on and the staff charts show regular checks. At one point you said your right arm hurt just below the shoulder, so I put ointment on it. I did see what looked like a faint bruise there, so maybe you had banged it on something.

Your aide came in and ordered your supper tray to be delivered to your room. You dozed a little, then asked if you were supposed to do something with vegetables.

I said, "do you mean like gardening?"

Then you said, "It was more like shopping."

I mentioned that maybe they talked about shopping or maybe you were just dreaming about it.

You replied, "There's always that." Then you said you don't shop anymore.

I said, "No, you don't have to. You get served here," which you agreed was a good thing because you don't cook anymore.

At about 4:15 PM you took your O^2 off. I asked why and you told me it was bothering the back of your neck. I thought it might be too tight. I brushed your hair and put it back on you a little more loosely. You said that was better.

At about 4:50 I called the Hospice nurse because you said your right shoulder was hurting and was not working when you tried to pull your pants up after using the toilet. Your nurse suggested asking you if you need a pain pill. Your response was, "Not really." She suggested putting ice on it. Tomorrow, your visiting nurse will assess your right shoulder.

While still on the phone, I asked the Hospice nurse to include a note about your rash and to talk to Glenda about alternatives for Lorazepam. She agreed and also said it would be good to put on a good coating of Desitin® each time we help you clean yourself up in the bathroom.

We are going to ask the staff to assist you with your toileting and O^2 during the hours when we are not here. You are no longer able to pull the cord for assistance on your own.

Your supper arrived at 5:15 PM. You ate only a few bites of carrot, egg casserole and a few spoonfuls of soup before you said you were too full to eat anymore. You did eat your dessert and drank your chocolate milk. You said later that nothing sounded appetizing to you.

I asked, "Not even ice cream?"

You replied, "No, not right now."

After supper I helped you get cleaned up and ready for bed. Your aide said that they do offer to help you in the bathroom, but that you usually refuse. She did say she will offer when she checks on you later.

We helped you out of your clothes, into your magenta nightshirt and bed. I read to you from the *Proof of Heaven* book. It looked like you had fallen asleep but if I stopped reading you would open your eyes, so I continued.

Then you would fall asleep so I would write in your journal. Shortly after I stopped reading, you would open your eyes and say something about the story. Sometimes I would continue reading. Sometimes I would just talk to you about it until you fell asleep again.

By 7:30 pm you were sleeping soundly, or so it seemed. You kept opening and closing your eyes again like you were trying to stay awake. You suddenly sat up and fiddled with the sheets. I helped you straighten them and you laid back down.

The med aid came in and gave you your glaucoma eye drop at 7:40 PM. I finished telling you the story of *Proof of Heaven*, and said good night to go home at 7:45 PM.

March 19, 2013
Glenda's entry

When I arrived at 11:40 AM you were sleeping in your red chair. You roused when I came in. Your Hospice nurse arrived around noon.

We discussed your agitated reaction to the Lorazepam. She will write orders to discontinue that and use Haldol instead. It will not react with the Oxycodone.

Your O^2 levels were at 82% after being without your supplemental oxygen for a few minutes. They returned to 96% as soon as I put your oxygen back on. Your lunch tray came at 12:30, but you only ate a few bites of soup before you needed to go the bathroom.

After, I helped you get cleaned up. Your nose was really runny so you kept taking off your O^2 to blow it. Between that and the exertion of getting to the bathroom you were very sleepy. By the time you got back to your chair, you nearly fell asleep in your lunch.

You awoke enough to eat a few more bites of soup, but skipped eating any veggies or rice and went straight to the butterscotch pudding (of course).

I was playing the *20ᵗʰ Century Music* from the Reader's Digest CD, which you really seemed to enjoy. So we propped up your feet and you napped in your red chair. After your nap, I helped you transfer to your bed because you looked uncomfortable.

You fell sound asleep immediately. Your touch massage therapist arrived shortly after. You were so out of it that you really didn't know she was there.

You slept until Mother Nature urgently insisted a bathroom trip was necessary. As soon as were you back in bed you said you needed to have another BM, but then you went to sleep. When I arrived you were wearing your pretty new night shirt so you probably won't be getting dressed today.

Two hours later, we headed into the bathroom again. After potty chores, you sat in your walker and let me push you back to your bed. You are very tired and seem uncomfortable, but no specific complaints. You are just worn out.

By 3:40 you were restless again and complaining of hip pain.

I helped you transfer back to your red chair to see if a different position would help. You were tapping your feet to the music of a string orchestra playing old songs like, "By the Light of the Silvery Moon." You really seemed to enjoy that.

4:00 PM back to the bathroom. We are going to have the staff hold your daily laxative dose of Senna. It's proving to be a bit too effective. After the potty stop, we got you back into your red chair. You seem quiet, very tired, but lucid. You rocked to the music with your eyes closed while I read the *Cat Who* book to myself.

4:30 and your tummy is telling you it's supper time. I gave you a yogurt to get you through until your supper tray is delivered. I need to remember to always ask them to bring yogurt with your tray so that you will have a snack between meals.

5:20 I helped you get situated in your red chair with your table tray in front of you and went to heat my food in your little kitchenette. I guess you got tired of waiting for supper because when I came back into the main room you had put yourself back to bed.

5:30 You started having mild hallucinations. Your food tray finally arrived so we sat on the bed and I helped you eat. You were having a hard time recognizing utensils. I coached you through eating your stew. You had only two bites of stroganoff, guess that wasn't very appealing. You finished your chocolate milk and ate your entire caramel flan.

After supper, you started thinking that your sheets were a coat. It was hard for you to realize what they were so I answered your questions about the bed and sheets every five minutes for a bit. Then we tended to your usual evening ablutions. You had a hard time recognizing where the bathroom was. We got you into bed and you had your eyes closed within five minutes. Just a minute or two later you sat up and said in your agitated voice,

"Have I been put to bed?"

I wasn't sure what you meant until you said that when we were little, we liked to stay up so we had to be put to bed.

I said, "No, you just seemed tired so I helped you get in bed."

Then you laid back down and closed your eyes. I was getting ready to leave when you woke up a bit restless. Your staff caregiver came in then. We started talking about Kansas tornadoes. We grew up with them so they were no big deal to us. However, she was not used to them. While on vacation in Grand Junction, CO, the warning sirens sounded when she was on the toilet. It scared everything right out of her. We all had a great laugh over that!

Then you got up and started wandering around your room with two pairs of shoes in your hands. I figured out that you needed the bathroom. You were having trouble recognizing where the bathroom was. I put your slippers on your feet and helped you to the toilet. Then I put your blue shoes over by the AC unit with your other favorite shoes.

I helped you with the necessary clean up afterward. I coached you through washing your hands, and helped you find your way back to bed. Nothing seemed familiar to you. You couldn't figure out where you were sleeping. When I got you back in bed you didn't know what your pillow was.

You said, "What good is it? It doesn't give you anything."

Then I realized that your hip was really painful as you were finally able to say that it was screaming. I asked the med-aid to bring you an oxycodone, but they are short staffed and still have quite a few members out sick from the Norovirus. It will be a bit before they can get it to you. Your next dose of Tylenol® and your sleeping pill won't arrive until around 10PM and it's only 6:30.

I think your confusion was exacerbated by your hip pain and by what is called, "Sundowner's Syndrome." People with Alzheimer's or other dementia tend to get more forgetful, confused, agitated and/or delirious after the sun goes down. You certainly seem to be following that pattern.

I rubbed the Chinese herbal pain gel on your hip and you were finally able to close your eyes. I will try leaving at 7:30. I alerted the staff that you were confused. I told them you had orders for Haldol and to give it to you if your confusion continues. Hopefully, you will sleep more comfortably now until your 10 PM meds arrive. The staff promised to check on you frequently as soon as it's quiet for the night.

Happy Spring! March 20, 2013
Glenda's entry

It's Equinox today! The seasonal change was ushered in with high winds and bursts of hard rain in big swirls of sunshine and stormy clouds. I arrived just before noon to find you sound asleep. You sat up for a moment, but you were pretty sleepy still. I sat on the bed with you and held you for a few minutes. But you were slumping forward so much I had you lay back down, which you were happy to do.

Lunch was interesting. It was meatloaf with mashed potatoes, but no gravy. You are supposed to be on a "wet food" diet as your mouth is too dry these days for you to swallow comfortably. The cauliflower was also plain and they forgot your dessert. You had about two bites of each item and turned up your nose. I gave you a yogurt, which you really enjoyed.

You went back to bed after supper feeling grumpy and out of sorts. Somehow, I figured out that discussing your diet needs with your caregiver bothered you. I realized it was because you felt your choices are being made for you.

So I sat on your bed with you and explained again about Hospice and that all of these people coming and going are just here to make your life as easy and comfortable as possible. That seemed to help.

You are fairly lucid today and ambulating to the bathroom easily. Sometimes it's hard for you to differentiate between the soap and the lotion dispensers by your bathroom sink. I cannot imagine what it must be like for you to have such a cloudy mind that it's hard just to wash your hands.

You also keep wondering what your bed sheets are – you keep thinking that they form a coat rather than your bedding. You've stayed in bed most of the time so far, not really wanting to sit in your red chair.

Today, we are listening to the *Stardust Moods CD*. It's a *Reader's Digest* compilation of string orchestra music. You seem to find the instrumental versions of songs like, "Some Enchanted Evening" to be very soothing.

You've only had one mild hallucination when you asked me what the writing on the floor reads. I answered, "Well, I think it's just shadows of light and dark," since I couldn't see what you are seeing. You seemed okay with that answer.

I think about you often when I am not here. I didn't sleep well last night and I went food shopping this morning, so I am really tired. I chose not to use my scooter since it was so wet and blustery out I just didn't want to bother with it.

That was a mistake. I barely made it through the check stand and came near to collapsing. A store staff member kindly brought me one of their scooters and helped me get the groceries in my car.

I am, therefore, very glad it's a short day for me as your Hospice volunteer will spend the afternoon with you. If I don't recover after resting at home for a bit, I will probably have to cancel attending my women's group tonight.

March 21, 2013
Glenda's Entry

You had a bath today so I'll give you a haircut after lunch. It is nice to see you up and dressed. You ate a bit more lunch than you have been eating lately, though they forgot your dessert again.

After your haircut, you were really tired. You had been without your supplemental oxygen during the trim. Your O^2 sats stayed in the low 90's. Still, that's a definite improvement from when they dipped to 82 without your oxygen for just a few minutes.

You are now relaxing and listening to tunes while sitting in your yellow rocking chair. Your volunteer said that you were singing with her yesterday. That makes me smile!

You are more lucid today than you have been recently. The only thing you've mentioned is seeing something flying over on your closet door. You tried telling me something when I was looking for your back scratcher, but it was just a string of non-related words so I never understood what you meant.

I put lotion on your itchy skin and we changed you out of your pants and a shirt and into a day dress because pulling your pants up and down every time you have to go the bathroom is wearing you out.

At 4PM you began having mild hallucinations. As you were sitting in the antique rocker across from your bed, you saw numbers like 47, etc. written into your pillow. You asked me what they were for.

I said, "Maybe it's shadows."

It's the only response I could think of. We enjoyed a cup of herbal tea together and you rocked quietly with your eyes closed until your afternoon yogurt snack at 4:30.

At 5:30 you went to the bathroom then blew your nose. Your O^2 sats dropped to 88 even though your oxygen was only off of you for two minutes. I replaced your oxygen tube, had you lie down and your sats came up to 98.

I stayed with you through dinner until you were resting quietly at 6:30 PM. Though I can't always follow where your mind takes you, I am glad I can be here with you.

Bye Mom. I sure love you!

Chapter 5

AND WE LAUGHED!

To truly laugh, you must be able to take your pain, and play with it!

~ CHARLIE CHAPLIN

y mom was intelligent and charming with a laugh that once heard, few forgot. Laughter is a tradition in our family that started with our father's amazing ability to laugh hilariously at himself and sweep us along with him. The Rueger women have carried on bathing generously in whatever humor we can find in the moment. That sense of humor has held our family together through the many patches of unhappiness we've had to bear.

As I watched my mom slip away daily into the mucky mire of Alzheimer's confusion, we all grasped onto any rope of laughter we could find. And for that moment when my mom threw her head back and burst forth in loud guffaws, I saw the whole of her shining through again.

Witnessing those moments are why I refused to be anywhere else but by her side through this bizarre, confusing, end of life journey. That sense of levity helped us cope as we followed Mom through the strange wanderings of her increasingly confused mind.

If you feel challenged to understand why I chose to include some of these stories in this chapter on laughter, Charlie Chaplin already explained it. It takes a bit more effort to find the humor in uncomfortable, emotionally painful, situations. I recommend it anyway. A little levity brings some sanity to the insanity.

Emergency Room Fun – Flirty, funny mom strikes again!

Well, it's about 7 PM and Donna and I are with you in the emergency room. Your lungs sounded very rattly when I put my ear to your back. You are definitely not feeling well.

While in the ER they gave you a breathing treatment and you seemed to improve. But the real improvement came when you set eyes upon your handsome, young male nurse. To determine if you met the medicare requirements for admission, they needed to see how your oxygen saturation levels would perform while you were up and walking.

Mr. Handsome appeared and exclaimed, "Would you like to go dancing with me?" Donna and I exchanged wide-eyed grins as you suddenly took on the demeanor of a young teenager in the throes of her first crush.

He made jokes about waltzing away with you as he assisted you down the hall and back. Once your dancing partner nurse got you back to your ER gurney and tucked in, you turned to Donna and me exclaiming with flirty eyes and girly grin,

"I like my new home!"

We couldn't help ourselves and burst into laughter with you. Watching you reclaim your youthful, fun countenance helped us survive the hours of drudgery as we awaited test results and Doctor's orders. Fortunately, your O² levels remained high so they released you and you recovered at home with bed rest.

A little bathroom humor

Strangely, some of my most precious fun-filled moments with Mom happened in the bathroom while she was busy on the toilet. One afternoon I glanced at myself in the mirror while accompanying her as she answered her body's needs.

I said, "I'm so weird. I have a tiny little head, tiny little feet but my middle seems disproportionately big!" Then I told Mom that my husband always says my feet are so small because they grew in the shade of my rather large bosom. Mom totally burst into loud, gut laughter! We both laughed so hard we squeezed joyful tears from our eyes.

I loved those moments hearing her beautiful laugh. When sparked, her sense of humor remained vivaciously alive. In spite of everything, we still had laughter. I'll always be grateful for that.

Peeing Moments

Humor provided the opportunity to turn embarrassing, debilitating body function breakdown into bonding moments. As Mom's body grew weaker, she had no strength to move from the bed to the commode right next to it. In addition, her Alzheimer's weakened brain stopped communicating with her feet. She was no longer able to navigate a turn. Even with all three of us lifting, we were unable to get her in the proper position to sit on her commode. The only alternative was to encourage her to just let go and use her Depends.

Her mind simply could not accept that. After two or three tries without success, we all sat with her on the bed and told her to just let it flow... to no avail. So we began singing children's tunes with a few word changes.

Tinkle tinkle little star
helps you pee right where you are

And sung to Paul McCartney's, "Let It Be" was
"Let it pee, let it pee, it's okay right where you are, just let it pee!"

and

"The more we pee together, together, together,
the more we pee together,
the happier we'll be!"

Laughing together seemed to help you feel less embarrassed. Though, I think you finally reached down into that wellspring of stubborn will. With mighty effort from all of us, you made it onto the commode at last.

Humorous Authors to the Rescue!

We read aloud to keep Mom in a present moment more in alignment with our own. Aside from Lillian Jackson Braun's *Cat Who* mystery books, we also enjoyed Janet Evanovich's hilarious Stephanie Plum series. The escapades of a rather clumsy, female bounty hunter as she attempts to drag her various miscreants to justice provided daily doses of humor.

I highly recommend reading comedy books aloud, or to yourself.

It was one of our best anchors against the storm of emotions inherent in caregiving a loved one with Alzheimer's.

Donna's entry from that day noted that she read the last story in a novel called *Motherhood is Murder* by Diana Orgain. This crime-solving, new mom's antics provided another hilarious distraction.

Donna wrote, "Mom really liked the story. But of course, when I finished reading she got a bit mixed up and asked me what time the police were coming here."

June Fire Drill Gone Awry

"Good grief!" That's one of Mom's favorite expressions, and it definitely applies to today. The facility attempted to do a fire drill. What a disorganized mess that was! Had it been a real fire, we'd all be dead. The fire alarm sounded while Mom was on the toilet. I poked my head into the hall. One of the staff personnel said I needed to get her to the dining room area as soon as possible.

I headed back into the bathroom and tried to hurry Mom along, which never works. After much insistent cajoling, I finally got her dressed and loaded into her Royal Chariot and myself onto my scooter. As we began our mobility vehicle parade out of the door, a different staff member exclaimed that the fire drill is only for the North side of the building. Mom lives on the South Side.

I decided that since we were already loaded up, we would progress to the dining room for refreshments. I got iced lemon water and Mom got hot lemon tea. Beverages in hand, we turned our scooters back toward her room.

We had gone only a few feet down the hallway when we encountered a very frazzled, caregiver shouting instructions to go back to the dining room. On our way back, another staff member appeared repeating the original instructions that the drill was only for the North side.

Turning once again, and feeling like ducks in a carnival, we finally headed back to her room with our refreshments. We passed several staff members along the way. They were all mumbling and shaking their heads in complete confusion.

"Good grief," says Mom yet again.

Star-Crossed Lovers

My sister Donna wrote the next entry. I think my mom was quite a romantic and must have been a pretty adorable little flirt in her youth. No wonder she caught my dad's eye!

June 2, 2013 ~ Donna's Entry

I arrived at 12:45 PM today. Mom is lucid now and knows who I am. She thanked me for coming to spend some time with her. Of course, she does not remember that one of us is here every day. She is very grateful when reminded or informed of it.

She also told me in a confidential tone that she has a boyfriend here. "He worked here so the time he could spend with me was limited. I don't know if we still spend time together because now I can't remember," said Mom.

Present Day Reflections

I think Mom was referring to the previous summer when she'd had quite a fantasy about one of the young male caregivers. She called me one Sunday morning while I was out tending to our garden to tell me that she was getting married.

"Oh really," was my calm reply while inside my mind exploded with "WTF!"

She had fixated so much on a young man who worked there it was in the best interest of all for him to stop attending to her. Hormones are hormones and contrary to current cultural view they don't dissipate just because your skin's a bit saggier.

While it might seem a bit maudlin to include this story in a chapter about laughter, it still offers some insightful gifts. I chose to include the story because it was interesting to catch a glimmer of the flirty young woman she must have been and to honor her reemergence. Even in the uncomfortable parts of her Alzheimer's progression, there were gems delivered from her soul still fighting to express itself.

It helped me to look for the humor when I was confronted with her difficult to understand, eccentric behavior. It was a matter of catching sight of those soul gems in between the lines of what I found uncomfortable.

Over time, those fantasies faded away into the indefinable gray of her confused world. The idea that Mom's mind was acting out her fantasy lover scenario was disconcerting. Never the less, it was also a glimpse into her flirty, youthful self. I liked seeing that little peek into her inner world regardless of feeling sad because of her confusion.

The most important thing I observed as I traveled this incredible death walk with Mom is that what a soul most wants, even through the haze of confusion, is to be heard.

Too Stunned for Words

Learning how to respond to mom's very changeable reality was an interesting dance for us. Most of the time, I just said, "Okay" to whatever reality she presented. However, I failed miserably the day I finally figured out that when she was asking about how the doctors were going to handle her care, it became very obvious that she thought she was in labor.

I exploded with an incredulous, "You think you're pregnant!"

I was so shocked I honestly had no clue how to respond. Later, I laughed with my sisters over my stunned response. As I think about it now, I realize that she was in labor – just a very different kind.

Two days later, Mom began the final leg of her death walk. For the remaining ten days of her life, the three of us were pretty much camped out in her room at all times. In the beginning, it felt like we were kids on vacation again. I was thrilled to have us all together for an extended period.

As the days wore on and the stress mounted, there were definitely snippy, gnashing of teeth moments. Realization was dawning to us that Mom's exit was near. We would gripe at each other as the emotional and physical fatigue and exhaustion began to take it's toll. Yet even then, what could we do but laugh at ourselves! Laughter was always our way out of strife and back to connection with each other.

No Spoilers!

Sherry hates to have the end of a book discussed before she has read it herself. She is adamant about NO SPOILERS! One afternoon, Donna and I were discussing the latest Stephanie Plum escapade, which Sherry had not yet read. She made it clear that we were not to give anything away.

I was lying on one of the uncomfortable sleeping stations we had set up around the room as Donna let slip some clue to the end of the story. Sherry proceeded to launch into a vehement tirade of objection to having any details of the story prematurely revealed. I was attempting a peaceful moment of rest and there seemed no end to the vehement tirade.

I piped up with, "Okay, okay, Little Miss Bossy Pants, we get it!"

Sherry ceased her cranky monolog for a stunned moment before commencing a giggling fit, in which we all joined gleefully. Little Miss Bossy Pants proceeded to nickname Donna as the Know it All. She named me Miss Too Big for Her Britches. Mom had often called us that when we bucked her parental authority as children.

Giggles crescendoed into uncontrolled, slap-happy cackles. I wondered what the neighbor's thought as, no doubt, they heard our raucousness through the walls.

The Sleeping Station Comedy

We also engaged in uproarious laughter the day we decided to name our three lovely sleeping stations. Choice number one, previously known only as the Red Chair, became the Stubborn Chair. It is a recliner, which for some reason now refuses to recline. You can extend it fully back, flip up the foot rest and settle in for a comfy snooze. Best nap quickly, because within a few brief moments you will find yourself once again in an upright position.

For Donna and Sherry who are taller than me, it might take a bit before they found themselves fully upright rather than peacefully reclining. I, however, am very short and there is not enough of me to weigh the top half of the chair down. When I attempted reclining, I was nearly catapulted upright as if on a summer carnival ride. Sleeping? I don't think so!

Stubborn Chair morphed into Torture Chair as the nights wore on and we struggled to find a comfortable position while it attempted to launch us out of itself.

Sleeping station number two was an older, much used Nikken magnetic mattress pad. When placed upon Mom's unpadded carpeted floor, it became known as the torturous Bed of Rocks.

The magnets that were supposed to relax and soothe our aching back muscles instead felt like we were sleeping on small stones. To accompany this lovely sleeping pad was the Nikken pillow, aka the Granite Slab. Excellent for creating headaches!

Sleeping station number three was the gel pad from Mom's bed before Hospice provided her with a new, luxurious, air-cushioned mattress. We named this station, "The Deep Pit." It was so compressed in the middle from years of use that trying to climb out of it with our rather middle aged, aching bodies nearly required the assistance of a pulley system.

There was simply no easy or graceful way to haul oneself into an upright, standing position and our bones creaked in slow-moving protest. The accompanying pillow was a minimally softer version of the Granite Slab. It paired perfectly with the Deep Pit for maximum discomfort.

We had another few moments of neighbor disturbing, loud guffaws as we played with the creative names and descriptions of these, dramatically uncomfortable, sleeping stations.

Her Quick Wit Still Shines

One of my final and fondest humorous moments came on one of Mom's better days. She didn't spend much time sharing about her past. For some reason, that day she mentioned to her visiting hospice nurse that she once played the Cello.

Suddenly her humorous charm burst forth. She sat on her bed enthusiastically pantomiming her cello playing experience, complete with knees spread in proper instrument accommodating position. Her performance was like the sun of my mom's natural wit bursting through. We all roared in joyful response!

Mad, gleeful giggles are the perfect pressure relief valve! I advise generous doses daily. As the days rolled on, at some point in her journal I wrote, "We are not shy with our laughter. We are not trying to be quiet. Mom is in her own world now. We hope that hearing our laughter makes the part of her that is still within hearing range of us smile, too."

Chapter 6

LET IT FLOW
LIKE WATER

> **"But she wasn't around, and that's the thing when your parents die, you feel like instead of going into every fight with backup, you are going into every fight alone."**
>
> ~ MITCH ALBOM, FOR ONE MORE DAY

This chapter title references one of the messages I clearly heard from my Angel guides when I was in my mid thirties. They were telling me that I tended to hold emotional pain from the past in my body and that it was time to let it flow through me. To which I queried, "How do I do that?" Their answer was that I only needed to, "Let if flow like water gently down the hill."

That was a milestone moment for my journey to internal peace. I've been attempting to master that for the past twenty years. Sometimes, I even get it right. Though Mom's journey is all done, I am still learning from her. I've come to value the harsh lessons, too. They are an important part of our story.

Excerpt from my Personal Journal
January 9, 2015

You've been gone from this world for two years and six months. I seem to be very weepy today. I am feeling your loss so keenly it's like shattered glass has blown a hole in my center. This past December felt so different than from years past. Our parents, the foundation of us, are gone. We are the Elders now.

I watched the movie of our childhood Christmases I made last year in your honor and to honor the memory of our ancestors. I am sad, perhaps, because all that we were as a family together on those joyous mornings will never be again.

As I watched the first clip, I loved seeing your smiling face. You were a young mom showing off your Christmas presents for the camera. Donna was only a little over two months old. Dad looked so tickled! He couldn't stop touching her fingers and toes.

The faded, old movie colors couldn't dull your lovely, shiny, red hair. What a beautiful young woman you were! I could see the wonder of your hopes and dreams in your eyes and the joy of you and Dad as brand new, young parents.

I'm glad you did not know then all that would befall you as you moved through your life. How could you have known all of the family turmoil you would have to endure?

Perhaps, even worse is that who you were; your brilliant scientific mind, your charm, wit and unmistakable laugh, would slowly disappear into the black hole of Alzheimer's long before your body was done with you.

As your failing heart began to signal defeat, your physical strength and vitality were draining away like a faucet no one could shut off. How relieved I am now that your pain, confusion, and struggles are all done.

I remember during your Last Rites gathering. We sang, "All My Trials Lord will soon be over" to you even as you were unconscious. I wanted your trials to be done for you then. I wanted you to find restful peace.

And in all honesty, I wanted our trials to be over as well. I wanted relief from the stress of leaving our lives behind to sit vigil by your bedside for ten solid days. I was worn out as well from all that went before.

Becoming your parent required making hard decisions like taking away your financial independence and turning in your driver's license when Alzheimer's took over your brain. It was hard watching you go through things that I couldn't change or make easier for you.

I do know what it is to be a mom though I have born no children myself. I cleaned your poopy diapers, fed you when you couldn't feed yourself. I comforted you as best I could. Though, I often felt that I could never give enough comfort to make this dying thing any easier for you.

Still, we were together and real and honest with each other. Those moments brought me more joy than was stolen by the total of all of the combined pain, hurt, anger, and sorrow of our lives.

Facing the world without you now is weird. I feel like something is out of place, and I can't quite make it right. Those who only knew you in your bitter years do not understand why I still grieve for one who seemed so harsh. I lost boyfriends because they couldn't tolerate your bitterness. And yes, I had my healing work to do from the times when your inner uglies made you cruel and hurtful to your young daughter.

By the age of seven, most of the physical abuse had long since ceased. Still, it took me years to forgive how harshly you sometimes treated me for no reason that I could comprehend. Do you remember the time I was just finishing my after school chore of doing the breakfast dishes? I was still rinsing my hands in the lukewarm water while you shoved passed me and turned the water to full hot while my hands were still under the faucet.

When I protested with an, "Ow, Mom, you burned me!"

Your only response was, "tough!" Internal scars can hurt far longer than external ones.

The important thing for me is that there in those last days, I again saw glimpses of the woman who had also nurtured me, loved me and was my close friend. There were moments of lucidness when the good mom you had been shined through the Alzheimer's veil.

May 29, 2013
Glenda's Entry

As I enter the room, I notice that you are all fresh and clean from your shower earlier this morning. I am thrilled to observe you sitting on your bed alert, perky and lucid. The mom I once knew is beaming at me through bright eyes.

As we go through our afternoon routine together, all of the care you need is taking its toll on me. My weak body suddenly collapses. As I struggle to stand you ask, "What happened?" Though I've had this mitochondrial condition for a few years now, to you it's like the first time you've known about it.

I patiently explain that the condition causes extreme fatigue with minimal activity. My legs buckle without warning, and it's hard to breathe because my muscles can't keep up with the demands of my lungs. You encourage me to sit beside you on the bed.

Suddenly, I am pulled nearly onto your lap in the warmest, tightest embrace we've had for years. Snuggling me tightly, you whisper "Dog gone it!" in my ear as you did when I was little and crying over some insult or injury. I surrender into your embrace and let the tears roll down my face. I deeply cherish this moment. I know it's the last time that instead of a caregiver, I'll be just a daughter enfolded in the comfort of her mother's arms.

Present Day Reflections

I say to those who only knew your, grumpy, elderly, Alzheimer's self, "Yes, it's true. She was a bitch." I was often so angry and frustrated with you myself that I wanted to tear my hair out. Oh, I knew well your acid tongue in my growing years. Sometimes, I hated you for your bitchy moodiness and for abandoning me so totally when you went back to work after our move to Kansas City.

How could you have known that was the beginning of some of the loneliest times of my life? You were already gone in the morning when I awoke, and lost yourself in TV land at night. It seemed there was no room in your world for me then.

We continued muddling on through the weirdness of our family dysfunction. Dad had disappeared into a Darvon drug-induced stupor. You were either working during the day or lost in TV at night. Donna and Sherry also struggled to adjust to all of the changes. Dad's heart attacks and subsequent heart disease overshadowed the following years.

You struggled on as a full-time career mom with a sick husband, two teenagers and me. I felt lost in lonely, school-hating despair. Somehow through all of that, you and I found our way past the underlying tension, frustration, and anger that often permeated our home. We found our way into a real friendship.

I'll always remember the season tickets we enjoyed at Kansas City's Starlight Theater. Warm, summer Midwest nights are magical, and I loved sharing them with you. You gave me my love of theater and music.

I remember in ninth grade I used to call you between classes from the lobby pay phone while you were at work (no cell phones in those days). We would discuss what you might want for dinner and how our respective days were progressing.

As I hung up the phone, another student who had been waiting to use it asked me if I had been talking to my best friend.

I replied, "No. I was just talking to my mom."

Her jaw dropped as she exclaimed, "I would *never* talk to my mom like that!"

I felt then that our bond had become something out of the ordinary. We had become a buoy to each other through the tangled roots of our family sorrows.

Today, sitting in the midst of a noisy coffee shop, your laughter echoes in my mind. I send you a quick mental hug. I am aware that the hard times we lived through molded the comfort of our closeness. Everything we survived helped me develop the coping skills I still use today.

Taking a sip of my cappuccino, I reflect on that last moment of lucid tenderness we shared. I realize it wasn't easy to make the choice to love. Finding the place inside where I could love you Bigly required great courage and inner strength. I had to reach down deep into my inner core, to the place inside where I connect to something much bigger than myself. I had to be willing to fight my way past my anguish and anger to get to my ability to love Bigly!

Excerpt from my Personal Journal
Tuesday, May 24, 2013

I met today with our Hospice counselor. I'm so grateful that counseling services are part of the Hospice experience. I gained so much clarity. I had begun praying for an end to Mom's suffering some time ago. It was difficult to watch her be so miserable with physical pain and mental confusion. This session helped me realize that I've been trying to protect Mom. I have to let that go and get out of the way to give her the dignity of her own process.

During the session, I had a strong sense that Grandmother was present in the room with us. Her message, "You are caretaking your Mom's soul as much as her body. You are healing my soul, too." I understood her message to mean that we were healing family patterns of neglect and anger that had been with us for generations.

As soon as I mentioned Grandmother's presence to my my counselor, she felt goosebumps all over as did I. It was another reminder that we were not going through this process alone.

After this session, I am praying for help in allowing Mom her own process. It is hers, after all, and in that regard, really not my business. According to the work of Byron Katie (thework.com), there are three kinds of business; yours, mine and God's. My nose only belongs in my business. This death experience is between Mom and God.

I am releasing my need to protect you, Mom, considering it's a futile effort anyway.

After my counseling session, I headed to your place. You are having a terrible day today and telling me how much you just want it all to end. I cry a little at that. I am focusing on being fully present with you until you can rest more easily with the help of your medication. As you napped, I simply relaxed into the stillness within me. I forgot to bring the book I've been reading with me today. It's okay. Sitting quietly in peaceful Presence is enough.

Excerpt from my Personal Journal
Tuesday, May 28, 2013

My healing work about mom continues. I'm holding an Aquamarine stone as I write this because it helps release old emotional issues, especially anger. Well, when it comes to my mom I can sure use all of the help I can get.

I've put myself in a catch 22 when it comes to her. Being her protector means I can't allow myself to feel my anger toward her. Now the time has come to get this energy out of my life and heal any remaining discord between us. All of these years I tried to love her better, to heal her heart, protect her from pain–never allowing myself my feelings of hurt and sadness. The little girl I was wanted so much more from her. So now I just need to sit with these feelings finally allowing myself to fully experience them.

I don't want to love my anger away, pray it away or have it blessed away. I want to give myself permission to yell, scream, cry and let my mom be fully accountable for her selfish meanness.

Mom had ample opportunity to forgive her mother, to heal herself and open her heart. But oh no, she chose to remain locked in petty jealousies holding grudges against her childhood family. She passed the scars of her unhealed anger onto her children.

Now she's dying. She needs more help than she ever has before. Right now, I just don't feel like being there for her. I don't want to make it easier for her. I want her to feel every painful, mean, hurtful, bitchy thing she ever did to her children and her husband.

MOM, YOU'RE A FUCKING, SELFISH, PETTY, JEALOUS, BIG BITCH AND PART OF ME HATES YOU FOR MAKING

MY EARLY YEARS SO DAMN PAINFUL. RIGHT NOW, I WOULDN'T TAKE AN OUNCE OF YOUR PAIN AWAY BECAUSE YOU FUCKING DESERVE IT!

Excerpt from my Personal Journal
May 31, 2013

It's an entirely new day. I let my anger have its voice. Then I recognized and released the part of me that had assigned myself the role of her protector. I let go and let myself rage at her – on paper anyway. And it's enough. Releasing all of those pent up feelings has freed up my energy in a huge way.

I found my inner child and gave her voice. After she had expressed all of her anger, I realized my whole energy has changed. I can be in the presence of Mom's pain-filled, confused state and not suffer with her anymore. What a huge relief!

I can totally allow her this experience without feeling the need to run interference for her, which was always pointless anyway. I don't feel I have to run away from her suffering.

In that freedom, I had so much more energy today! On my way home from her place yesterday, I felt a nudge from my Angel guides to stop at the thrift store in my small hometown of Lafayette. I thought I was looking for a chair, but instead found two white cabinets for my bathroom. I have wanted to change out the old cabinets that are too big for the small bathroom for some time. These cabinets were the very things I've been wanting.

I wanted to have the bathroom all done and reorganized by the time my husband came home from work. Perhaps it was the same kind of energy some women experience before the birth of their child called, "nesting." If you think about it, in a way, I am birthing

Mom over to the other side so maybe that is what happened – it seems like that.

Whatever the cause, my weakened body, which often can't climb two steps unassisted, managed to haul the two cabinets into the house, empty the old ones and pull them into the living room. I hauled the new ones in place and had the entire bathroom cleaned and reorganized before my husband made it home from work.

I DID IT! He was so pleased and amazed. I was awed that I mustered the physical energy and strength to accomplish it. I felt like I was moving with superhuman strength and speed. I kept saying to my body over and over, "don't give out on me yet – just a bit more to go!"

Whether it was the cathartic release of emotions that allowed for such a major shift and energy spurt or it was some type of spiritual nesting syndrome, I don't know. What I do know is that I now find myself at peace with Mom's death process.

I clearly see how my relationships with other women who are nitpicky and controlling were affected by my unhealed issues with her. Their behavior hasn't changed at all. It just doesn't bother me because I recognize it's not personal. I can remain centered and peaceful in their presence and even in Mom's presence, too.

As I sat in peaceful contemplation next to Mom after my session with the Hospice counselor, she stirred from her mindless wanderings long enough to say something profound. I don't even know what inspired her words.

Out of the blue, she said, "and what you learned today you will carry with you for the rest of your life."

WOW! I know because of this message that we are connecting on a soul level. Letting go of all of my resistance feels fantastic! I am incredibly grateful to her for doing this healing work with me in her way. Her body may be failing, but her spirit still shines!

And the bagpipes played

I received one other gift as I was driving home that day. Scottish bagpipes make the blood of my ancestors sing in my bones. They are magical to me.

I remember last year when my brother in law, Chuck, had moved into the active dying phase. Sherry called from his Hospice room and asked that Donna and I sit by the fire pit in my back garden and focus upon filling his room with peace.

We sat in silent darkness lit only by the moon, stars and the warm glow of the fire. The moment he crossed over I heard the sound of bagpipes playing as if carried by the wind.

In a tearful voice I exclaimed aloud, "the Ancestors are calling him home!"

The telephone rang a few minutes later to call us to Hopewell House for a ceremony to honor Chuck and his passing.

After my meeting with the Hospice counselor on the day when Mom uttered such profound wisdom even through the thick curtains of her Alzheimer's mind, I took a different route home than usual. Upon turning the corner, I noticed a Scottish bagpiper playing on the street in downtown McMinnville, Oregon.

Intrigued, I pulled over into the nearest parking spot and got out of my car to listen. I found a seat around the corner in a nearby sidewalk café. I called a close friend to tell her about my afternoon of superhuman strength. I told her that it felt similar to what I've heard about the nesting phenomenon. We laughed about the weirdness of it.

When the conversation ended, I walked back the few steps I had come to listen again to the bagpiper only to find that he had disappeared. I had never seen him before nor have I since. I felt then that Mom's time was drawing near. In fact, it was just one month away.

Chapter Seven

THE NIGHT CLOSES IN

"Life offers us few guarantees except death. Having advance notice of the inevitable journey gives one the chance to "pack" for the trip. Do not deny yourself these blessings by denying that you are going away."

~ BARBARA K ROBERTS

Excerpt from a Hospice article on Preparing for Approaching Death

Vision Like Experiences

The person may speak of or claim to have spoken to persons who have already died, or to see or have seen places not presently accessible or visible to you. This does not indicate an hallucination or a drug reaction. This person is beginning to detach from this life and is being prepared for the transition so it will not be frightening. Do not contradict, explain away, belittle or argue about what the person claims to have seen or heard.

By the first of June, Mom's hallucinations (or not, according to the above text) began signaling the arrival of her final days. One of my ancestors kept a daily diary for most of his adult life. He plainly knew that his long life was nearing the end. In the recent weeks before he passed, he wrote that he had seen his deceased wife standing across the pond from him.

June 5, 2013
Glenda's Entry

Mom is talking about seeing people opening a door that appears to be at the foot of her bed. She says they come in, stare at us and then leave.

She mentioned feeling she is someplace her body is not. She says it feels like her body is coming apart on her. Once she pointed to her neck and said, "I need a new power necklace."

Upon seeing my puzzled face, Mom tried to explain that she makes a power necklace, so they know whether she has enough power to speak. She mumbles about a lot of people showing up yesterday to install her power necklace. She fixated on that for quite a bit.

Mom doesn't recognize she's in her room. She seems to be worried about getting somewhere on time; asking where the car is, are all of the boxes packed, etc. She keeps trying to tell me something about being on the wrong side of the room and her bed sheets are torn in pieces, but I can't quite figure it out.

After supper, she starts trembling from head to toe. I have no idea how to help or what's happening. As I sit watching, the few minutes it takes seem to drag into endless time. Suddenly the trembling stops! She sits forward and with a forceful voice exclaims, "I need to go home!"

Sisters, I'm thinking the conveyor belt of my Bear dream just picked up major momentum!

From this point on, we were only able to record snippets here and there in her journal. Some entries were dated and others not. We stopped writing our notes in Mom's book to her because she was beyond caring. We began writing them to each other or just to document what we were witnessing.

June 7, 2013
Glenda's Entry

Mom's Hospice nurse said in a recent conversation that it looks like Mom is changing. They will be back tomorrow or Monday to examine her. She is resting more quietly now.

The following Saturday Sherry wrote that Mom pronounced,
"I'm ready to go home."
Sherry said, "We aren't going anywhere at the moment so you can just rest."
Mom repeated being ready to go home so, Sherry asked her, "Where is home?"
Mom told her that her home was in Pratt, KS. Sherry asked her if she could tell her about her home in Pratt, but Mom said, "It will take too long!"
As her fixation on going home continued Sherry said, "Do you remember the Wizard of Oz?" Mom told her she did.
Sherry told her, "Okay then, just be like Dorothy in the Wizard

of Oz. Just close your eyes and say, "I want to go home, and you can be there in your mind." So Mom closed her eyes and said, "Okay," though she was still too restless to sleep.

Shortly after that, Sherry asked Mom if she would like her to read allowed. Her reply, "Might as well, since I'm not making any headway with what I'm doing."

So Sherry read aloud from the *Proof of Heaven* book until Mom dozed. Once Sherry resituated Mom in bed with pillows propping her up behind her back, she finally slept.

June 10, 2015
Glenda's Entry

Oh dear, I was so intent on writing this note in the journal that I wasn't paying attention to Mom. I thought she was resting quietly until I suddenly looked up. She was toddling toward me naked from the waist down with a confused look on her face and a clean Depends in her hands.

I helped her change into her clean undies and the day dress with the lavender flowers and got her ready for a lie down. I washed her hands with the antibacterial wipes while she sat on the bed.

After she was resting quietly, I discovered she had dumped her wet underwear in the toilet. She knew something wasn't right, but didn't know what it was. That's why she came and got me. Goodness – must pay attention!

Later she said, "I just want to die!" I tell her that I understand. Mom mentions Dad quite often now. I actually find her conversations about him quite encouraging. I hope it's a signal that she will find her release soon.

4:00 PM – I checked Mom's O² levels. They were down to 87 so I increased the room diffuser to 4L. As the day wears on she continues to get weaker, yet even more restless.

The three of us struggle to assist her as her weakness increases. We get help and transfer her back to bed, but it doesn't matter where we put her, she won't stay still for very long. Propping her up with pillows is the best we can do. Her breathing is getting harder as her lungs fill with fluid.

Her Hospice nurse is ordering a switch to liquid morphine as soon as she can reach the doctor to sign the order. They are proposing to discontinue the Lasix, which will reduce the number of pills she takes. The potassium will be discontinued as well.

Her nurse is concerned that the Lasix is too taxing on her kidneys. She also advised that the death process is actually easier when the patient is dehydrated. It assists with a more peaceful passing. We are now giving Mom water only when she asks for it.

At 4:50 AM Mom woke up and was hungry so I fed her butterscotch pudding. Later, our Hospice counselor came for a visit while Mom slept and I went to the store. She told Sherry that she would ask the Hospice Chaplain to come by. He's known as the Singing Chaplain. He brings his guitar providing music and songs we can all sing to as he visits. Mom loves music.

Even though her sleep is getting deeper and longer and she often doesn't speak, we still have so many precious moments with her. Donna was trying to tell her not to worry.

Mom replied, "You're the one who's worrying. I'm just sitting here."

Still practical as ever!

When Donna gave her a bite of watermelon, her face lit up! Next came another of Mom's favorites, chocolate pudding. Donna barely had time to reload each spoonful before Mom would be anxiously opening her mouth for the next bite.

By the 19th, Mom became mostly non-responsive. As I was attempting to soothe my tired nerves by glancing out the window late that afternoon, I saw a crow fly past. The first crow landed on the lawn in front of Mom's room. Shortly, a second crow flew in and cawed once. Then they both flew away.

I've always had a special affinity with crows. They always appear when my life is about to change.

Chapter Eight

LAUGH AS WE
ALWAYS LAUGHED

**"Whatever we were to
each other, that we are still.
Laugh as we always laughed at the little
jokes that we enjoyed together. Play,
smile, think of me, pray for me."**

~ HENRY SCOTT HOLLAND

According to the information I found on the North Florida Hospice website, restlessness increases as our loved ones prepare to leave their body's behind. The article states, "The person may perform repetitive and restless tasks. This may, in part, indicate that something is still unresolved or unfinished."

Mom's restlessness increased. She was always fiddling with the bed sheets and making motions in the air with her hands as if she were picking or sorting things out. She started falling into longer and deeper sleep cycles. We continued to speak to her, read to her and sing to her.

June 17, 2013
Glenda's Entry

I brought Grandmother's Bible with me today. I read selections from Psalms because you said once again, "I'm tired. I wish I could just go."

I said, "I know. We are preparing ourselves for that. I would escort you there myself if I could. But it's not my job. That's between you and the Angels."

So I read all of the passages I could find relating to Angels and how they are here to help. I read the ones that encourage strength and the belief in a power greater than ourselves. In these words, I hope Mom finds comfort.

Mom's Hospice Volunteer took over her care that afternoon. She wrote:

"A restless afternoon. She sure is a tease! She was pretending to spit her mouthwash at me. She couldn't keep a smile off of her face! Glenda, she wants to know for sure that you were here today. She can't remember."

8:00 AM June 18, 2013
Glenda's Entry

We all slept! My husband, Mike, called. I had the sound on my phone turned down, so I barely heard the ring. It woke me up enough that when the med aide came in with her morning meds, I was up. Mom is off of Lasix now, so I refused the potassium as her hospice nurse instructed me to do. I also requested morphine. It seems to help.

Her Sacred Death Dance Carries Us in its Wake

We sisters were moving with Mom in a dance led by the sacredness of the moment. We were swept along in the flow of the dance leaving very little time for writing. I began randomly logging what I was witnessing as the scenes unfolded.

Mom is now totally bedridden and minimally responsive. Her staff caregivers came in and freshened her up. She was able to swallow pills on command and follow instructions while being changed.

She is coughing some, can't breathe easily and is in quite a bit of pain. I asked the med aide to bring cough syrup and morphine asap. She's stirring and very restless. Donna rubbed some Arnica gel on her back.

She's trembling and cold. We put her sweater on her and added the quilt though it didn't help. She's still trembling. We put her kitty-shaped neck warmer in the microwave to heat and then placed it on her neck and shoulders to help her relax and feel warmer.

We were able to get her to lean on propped up pillows behind her back. That helped briefly. She could only tolerate that position for five minutes. Now she wants to get up. Music helps, so I put on the Orca Suite CD. She likes that one better than the James Galway pan flute music. That one had more pop music on it than I remembered.

Her hands seemed constantly wanting to grab and twist the bed sheets as if they wanted to be busy. While on a supply run, I found a Kermit the Frog soft wrap meant for drying newborns after a bath. I thought having something soft to hold might be comforting to her.

At the store, I was unable to decide between Kermit and some other stuffed animal, so I bought them both. Mom's words were pretty much completely inaccessible to her at that point. However, she distinctly made her preference known by throwing the stuffed animal across the room. Kermit stayed tightly in her grasp for as long as her ability to hold on remained.

In his book, *Die Wise, A Manifesto for Sanity and Soul*, Stephen Jenkinson says that dying requires as much labor to get a soul to the other side as physical birth requires to bring a soul into this world. I hadn't known about his book then. I can say that what we witnessed lends credibility to this notion.

June 20, 2013
Donna's entry

Mom is now unable to swallow pills at all, so her nurse is discontinuing all pill medications. She instructed that we can ask for morphine in between the scheduled four-hour doses to help with her breathing challenges. She said that the cough is part of the dying process. She instructed us that repositioning Mom will help. The itching also seems to be part of the process.

While Glenda was out, Sherry and I gave Mom a tepid water bath and changed her into a clean nightshirt. It seems to have helped. Her Healing Touch massage therapist came to give her a last soothing massage and to say goodbye.

The Circle of Love Gets Bigger

As her time drew nearer, old family friends and current ones either called or emailed for daily progress reports. Members of our women's healing group were sending Reiki and prayer support daily. It was so comforting to know that we were held and encircled by the loving thoughts of our dear friends. A delivery of gluten free cupcakes from one of our women's group members was received with enthusiastic gratitude!

June 22, 2013
Donna's Entry

Earlier, we talked to our lifelong childhood friends John and Tyra Barnes. Tyra asked us to encircle Mom in our arms and tell her that they loved her and wished her a peaceful journey to the other side. We did as Tyra asked.

We sang a few verses of "I Love You Forever." She is very restless and fidgety. Her eyes are open but glazed. Her nurse assured us that, too, is normal. Her eyes are focusing on things we cannot see.

Sherry is sitting with Mom now, and she is calmer. Then Sherry took a shower, so I sang to Mom for a bit. She seemed to like that.

The Last Rites

As Mom slept one afternoon very deeply, Kathleen, Mom's Priest, came to deliver her Last Rites. The Singing Chaplain was there, and a few other friends stopped by to visit. We filled her room with voices raised in song and focused on her with total love.

After the singing, we told our favorite mom stories. It was good to hear from Mom's church members who had been praying for her.

Her hospice team members and volunteers who were there and her massage therapist all remarked how touched they were by Mom's charming, spunky personality and how she made them laugh.

Mom slept through the whole thing, but I am sure her inner being was well aware. I am glad that we were able to share that time with her. So, Mom, I continue to laugh as we always laughed and to say your name with no sorrow in my tone. We are all here with you until you have no more need of us.

Chapter 9

HER LAST HURRAH

"Why does it happen? I don't think anyone can say for sure, but in each case I witnessed, it gave the person who was dying an opportunity to say things to loved ones or to participate in the lives of their loved ones in some way that would otherwise not have occurred."

~ JANET MACKENZIE, ND

---

*T*he above quote is from an online discussion of a phenomenon often referred to as the final rally, or the Last Hurrah as I call it. Our loved ones seem to shed the effects of their illness and appear nearly normal for a brief time. They somehow muster enough strength to be once again fully present, and able to accomplish physical tasks previously impossible.

Tyra's sister, Rexene, is my best friend from childhood. Her husband died several years ago from bladder cancer. He had been very ill for some time. One day he announced that he wanted to go canoeing with her, always a favorite shared activity.

As they spent the day on the water together, she was thinking, "This is great! Maybe he's getting past this!" But at the end of the day, he was much weaker. Once back in bed, he slipped into a comatose like state for a time before his spirit left. What a gift for them to have had that last day together!

One of my current best friends just passed away recently. She had been in and out of the hospital for the two months prior. She was in ICU and had already coded at least once when she seemed to rally. She had a few happy hours with her daughters and family, a final phone call with me and then she, too, slipped back into a comatose-like state from which her body did not wake.

My brother in law was able to spend his last conscious day in energetic and animated conversation with Sherry, Donna, Bill and two of their closest friends.

When his hospice nurse asked if he was getting tired and wanted to rest, he replied, "No, these are my people!"

I would say this is a very real phenomenon of which we should be aware. If you are lucky enough to witness it, revel in it! Making that final connection seems crucial. In my opinion, this is a miraculous gift. It contains the last opportunity we have to connect soul to soul with our loved ones while they are still in this world with us.

Sunday, June 23, 2013
Glenda's Entry

It's my turn in the Torture Chair. I've been on duty since Donna went to lie down sometime in the wee hours of the morning. Sherry had the roughest of the day shift duties so we've been letting her sleep.

Donna rested on the Deep Pit to try and sleep. That leaves me half dozing from about 3 to 5 AM in the Torture Chair parked next to Mom's bed. She is actually kind of restless again and trying to climb out of bed.

I sit next to her and say in my tired, grumpy voice, "Mom, please, just let go. I wish you didn't have to struggle so hard." She grumbles something back, but I'm too tired to notice and move to the yellow rocker to see if I can rest better there.

A bit later, Donna is still lying on the Deep Pit gel pad on the floor, which affords her a perfect view of the room from underneath Mom's bed. Sherry is sleeping on the Bed of Rocks behind me. Suddenly, Donna sees Mom place one foot on the floor over by the Torture Chair and then the other.

Through my sleepy haze, I hear Donna say, "Mom, what are you doing?"

She replies, "Oh, probably something I'm not supposed to be."

I am up and fully alert in an instant. Donna and I exchange glances of surprise and wonder as we quietly watch. Mom, who has been in a nearly infantile, comatose and unresponsive state for the past few days, is now getting herself out of bed and transferred to the Torture Chair without any assistance. Dawn was just beginning to waken the sky.

Donna says, "Sherry, you might want to wake up now."

As mom sits in her chair, she sees us through eyes bright with life and total clarity, a soft smile warming her face. We three sisters move to encircle her, each of us holding her hands. We share how much we love each other and how glad we all are that we are family. We laugh at some of our favorite memories.

Then Mom says, "I've raised three beautiful daughters. My work is done."

As the day wore on, caregivers drifted in and out, and we shared many conversations with her hospice nurses. At about 1 PM, while she still had hospice visitors there, the candle flame snuffed out. All of the animation in Mom's eyes and gestures left. She sank back into a non-responsive state. It took four of us to get her out of The Torture Chair and back into bed. She was totally dead weight as if her spirit had already flown.

She remained in that state for the next three days. We sat constant vigil through the rest of that day and continued singing and talking to her throughout the night. Her body was still breathing, but it was as if she was gone.

The North Florida Hospice article states, "When a person is emotionally-spiritually-mentally resolved and ready for this release, but his or her body has not completed its final, physical shut down, the person will continue to live until that shutdown process ceases."

We sang every song we could think of and read comforting poetry aloud throughout the night. There were tears and some sharp words amongst each other as the strain and fatigue pushed us to our limits and emotions crescendoed.

Finally, at around 5 AM Monday morning we all surrendered to exhaustion. Sherry and I attempted sharing the very narrow Bed of Rocks. I ended up with my upper body mostly on the bare floor, too drained to notice or care.

On the morning of the 24th, Sherry is clearly exhausted. She lives the farthest away and has not been home for several days in a row. Since there is no further change in Mom's condition, Donna and I encourage Sherry to leave. She reluctantly agrees and heads home that afternoon to engage in some much-needed rest in a comfortable bed and to shower in her own, familiar place.

12:30 AM, Tuesday, June 25, 2013
Glenda's Entry

Donna and I notice Mom's body feels cold and clammy. This is another sign that she is in what hospice calls, "the active dying phase."

Mom's hypothalamus, the temperature regulating system, has shut down. Her fever spikes to about 102 degrees. Donna and I discuss whether we should call Sherry but decide it would be best to let her sleep longer as Mom's breathing is not changing.

We keep dousing Mom with soothingly cool, damp washcloths. We put them in her hands and under arms and on her face and neck. We called the hospice night nurse who confirmed that the temperature change is part of the dying process.

It is amazing how the mind can deny reality. I know mom is dying, but when I heard the rattly breathing my first thought was to get mom to the hospital to treat the onset of pneumonia.

The hospice nurse is very patient with me when I mention pneumonia. She confirms that the rattly breathing is part of the dying process. She says to turn her every four hours or so, and to keep washing her with a cool cloth. She told me to cover Mom only with a sheet and to keep the room below 70 degrees.

We called Sherry at around 8 AM. She was still asleep. Getting from her house to where we are is more than an hour-long commute. She needed to wake, eat, care for her cats, shower and repack. At about 11 AM, she came rushing in, unloaded her fresh supply of clothes and necessities and sat beside us to hold Mom's hand.

"I'm here, Mommy," she says. "I'm here."

Donna's son Adrian called. While Donna was speaking with him, Sherry said, "Mom, your grandson loves you and knows you love him, too."

She was able to say, "uh huh."

We were glad that she knew Adrian was on the phone. I don't remember her saying anything again.

As time melted on, the hour of the day was no longer definable. We were moving in altered time, sacred time. It was either light or dark outside, and that's all we knew. The following are my memories as they happened. They remain in my mind with the same clarity as if they had happened yesterday.

Unto Her Last Breath

On Wednesday morning, the 26th of June, my husband had most of his teeth pulled in preparation for dentures. Donna's husband Bill picked him up after the surgery and took him home. I lived only fifteen minutes away, so I went home to check on him.

Near 1 PM, I was getting ready to make myself some caffeine tea. I needed a boost for my return trip to Mom's apartment. Just as I put the kettle on, Donna called to say I needed to come back at once. I dropped everything and raced as quickly as possible back to Mom's side.

Her breathing had been extremely rapid through most of the morning. While I was gone it began to slow down. I was amazed at the change in the short time I was away.

Once back in her room, the three of us gathered tightly around Mom. I had crawled up onto the bed behind her. Donna and Sherry had each pulled the other two rocking chairs up next to the bed. We were all connected as we held onto mom. The time for songs was over. We simply sent her all the love we could muster.

Mom's eyes suddenly opened, looking around wildly, perhaps for a point of reference or reassurance.

Sherry spoke soothingly, "It's okay, Mom. We're all right here. We're right here with you."

Her eyes calmed and focused on Sherry, and then she seemed to relax into herself as I added, "And Dad and Grandmother and Granddaddy and your brothers and sister are all here, too, ready to greet you on the other side. It's okay to go now, Mom. We're all here, and we all love you."

Donna and Sherry joined in,

"We will always love you. Forever and ever. You will always be our Mommy."

At 2 PM, as I had my fingers on her carotid artery, I felt her pulse get slower and weaker until it finally just stopped. There were no bagpipes this time. Just silence.

Fighting back the tears, I called the front desk and asked for a nurse to come and do a vitals check. The nurse confirmed that Mom had finally embarked upon the journey for which she had been preparing.

The Final Goodbye

Our husbands Bill and Mike came. Mike appeared with teabags on his gums to quell the bleeding from his recent oral surgery. My dentist dad taught me that remedy. The hospice team came along with the with the Singing Chaplain. He brought his guitar, and we had a final goodbye with all of those present; our voices raised once again in prayerful song. The Chaplain led us through a beautiful prayer service.

The hospice team had cleaned Mom up and put her in a fresh, clean blouse. They lit battery operated votive candles and placed them by her bed. We sang songs and laughed again as we shared some of our favorite mom memories.

Bittersweet camaraderie filled the room. The big, deep Love that held us up through the worst of times made Its Presence known. After sharing more tears and hugs goodbye with those gathered, we were left alone to have a last, private moment with Mom.

When her final chariot had arrived to claim her body, we silently escorted her out of the building. We all watched as the attendant loaded her into the awaiting hearse. The long goodbye was finally over. Together, we had mid-wifed Mom on to the other side.

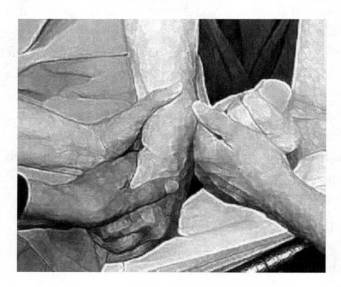

Chapter 10

SHE IS FREE

**And how else can it be?
The deeper that sorrow carves into your
being, the more joy you can contain.**

~ The Prophet by Kahlil Gibran

I sit in the garden on Thursday morning the 27th of June to soothe my exhausted body and soul. A gentle breeze pushes my hammock chair, and I suddenly feel Mom's presence. I feel my heart infused with love and gratitude. I hear a soft whisper float by on the wind, "Thank you for taking such good care of me. I love you."

And then she's gone. I saw a vision of her as she looked in college. Her lovely, red hair was long, shining and dancing in wispy feathers around her face as if in response to some gentle breeze. She smiled softly.

I remember during the last few days of our long vigil I was entering the building on my return from a final supply run. I passed another family gathered in conversation on the front patio bench. They were also visiting their loved one preparing to leave this world.

Their words were full of bitterness and hatred about some other sibling and how glad they were that the person in question was not coming.

I thought, "How sad. You are missing the magic of the moment when Love can steal away resentments and open your heart beyond all expectation." The only requirement is willingness. That kind of Love flies on its own wings.

Sherry and I had visited with our hospice counselor, Val, in the last weeks before Mom left us. Val told us that the previous weekend she had gone walking on the beach by the light of the full moon. She said she wasn't even in a work frame of mind when a strong compulsion nudged her into looking down at her feet. There in front of her were three, small, overlapping, oval-shaped stones worn smooth by the pounding surf.

Val thought, "those are for the Rueger sisters!" So she brought them home for us. At our meeting, she set them on the table before us along with a set of colored pens. She told us to pick one and sit in quiet contemplation for a moment. Then we were to write one word on the rock that would inspire us.

My word was, "Trust." Sherry's was, "Forgive." We gave Donna's stone to her when next we saw her. After a brief meditation, she wrote, "Perseverance" upon her stone.

With Trust, Forgiveness, and Perseverance we survived the extreme emotional highs, lows and the utter physical exhaustion of our long vigil with mom. We found the strength to conquer our reticence and handled the unpleasant, grueling tasks that are all part of being fully engaged in the care of a loved one through the dying experience.

Per the quote at the beginning of this chapter, sorrow did carve deep grooves on my soul, which then became the channels for Loving Bigly. I am in awe of all that I experienced in my life with

Mom. Even as I cry with my own loss and sadness, I cannot help but feel her joy. She is finally, truly free. There is nothing left but Love.

EPILOGUE

A Healing Journey

*F*or those of you who are familiar with Shamanic Journey work, you will understand the following experience known as a Soul Retrieval Journey. It is very similar to a technique used in Energy Psychology called Matrix Reimprinting.

These techniques allow us to access and free the unhealed parts of ourselves that are still frozen in past traumatic experiences as if locked in a time capsule. Even though my adult self had worked through her feelings and found peace with her mom, there was a part of me that had remained frozen in her lonely past.

I have often heard it said that personal growth work is like peeling the layers of an onion. It traditionally follows a spiral pattern. It is not unusual to have deeper layers of the same issue present themselves again, even though you may say to yourself, "But I've dealt with this issue!" Each layer often affords us a different perspective.

For those of you who may be unfamiliar with meditative journeys, they contain amazing healing opportunities. Shamanic Journey work, guided meditations, and other energy psychology techniques are simply maps we can use to access within ourselves all that keeps us trapped in negative emotion and self-limiting beliefs. The goal is to identify, unravel and clear them.

Energy Psychology methods can easily fit within any faith or life philosophy you currently practice. One of the techniques called,

"Emotional Freedom Technique" (aka EFT or tapping) specifically targets the deeper, core layers more rapidly.

Once cleared, memories of past traumatic events have no more negative charge. In my experience, the negative emotions find permanent release. There is mounting clinical evidence gained in documented research trials over the past several years to substantiate my results. You'll find a link to them in the Resource section.

Important note: EFT is not a replacement for traditional medical treatment methods. Rather, it works well as a complement to any care you may receive from your doctor or licensed clinical therapist.

As I've integrated these techniques into my daily life, I have found access to more healing, deeper love, and greater joy than I ever conceived could be. Though I continue to deal daily with the physical limitations of my body, I have been able to reclaim much of my stamina and have achieved a more fulfilling life. I feel I've stepped into fresh air and sunshine after being trapped in a dark, musty basement for a very long time.

This kind of healing work takes trust, forgiveness, and perseverance as my sisters and I found in our final days with Mom. It's also vital to include self-forgiveness generously. For maximum effectiveness, I recommend working with a trained professional to help you navigate your inner world with grace and ease.

Be open to your inner courage and have faith in the process. Imagine being handed a small acorn having never seen one before and hearing, "someday this is going to be the biggest, most beautiful tree you've ever seen."

All I can say is plant the acorn and watch what grows.

Excerpt from my Personal Journal
July 29, 2016

Yesterday, I had a Reiki healing session with a fellow Reiki/EFT Practitioner who is another visionary intuitive like me. During the treatment, she saw that I had built a barrier outside of my emotional energy field. She described it as looking similar to the big, white rental tents often seen at large outdoor events.

She explained that, though the doors had been tightly zipped, they were now open letting the breeze through. She then noticed a little girl standing outside the tent peeking in shyly.

I immediately knew it was the part of me that still felt lost in those lonely first years after our move to Kansas City. She wasn't sure she would be welcome if she came in. I visualized myself inviting her to climb up on the Reiki table with me and promised her that I would spend more time with her in future.

This morning as I sat in my garden, I started the daily five-minute energy routine as taught by Donna Eden (see Resource section for more information). I'd only progressed halfway through what she calls the Wayne Cook Posture, known for clearing emotion, when I became aware of Little Glenda's presence in my mind.

I began tapping to help my body cope with the sudden onslaught of emotion. Feelings of anger, hurt, and humiliation that had been stifled for years gushed forth in a torrent. While tapping, I reached out in my mind and heart center to connect to that young part of me still lost in the emptiness of those early days.

I visualized Little Glenda sitting across from me in the garden. I tapped the EFT points on her little body for her. I pulled her onto my lap and let her rant all of her feelings while I continued gently tapping on her.

I told Little Glenda to line up her entire family in front of her.

I let her yell and scream all that she wanted to say to her mom, dad and sisters. She cried about feeling so abandoned and unwelcome, scolded Mom and screamed at Dad for all of the pain they had caused her. She cried at Donna and Sherry for the times that they ganged up teasing her so mercilessly she wanted to disappear. She continued to pour out her hurt and anger until spent.

When she finished, I asked the family to respond to her by telling her what they loved about her. They offered these healing words:

Dad said he loved her adventurous spirit and willingness to be his fishing/photography buddy. He always looked forward to their outings together.

Mom loved her bright and fun loving spirit that she called her Little Snickelfritz.

Sherry loved her for being her friend and companion during her troubled times and for the friendship, and spiritual interests they shared after Donna left for college.

Donna admitted that she hadn't taken the time to get to know her then and apologized. But she knew that they would be great friends in the future and was very glad about that.

I finished the journey by asking Little Glenda to give each of them something to symbolize healing between them.

She gave Dad a yellow rose to express all of the friendship and fun adventures they had shared together. Yellow was always his favorite color.

She gave Mom a white rose to symbolize new peace between them.

Sherry got a red rose to show how deeply she loves her.

Donna's gift was a clear quartz crystal to add energy to her creative self-expression and her strong spirit.

Little Glenda was finally able to understand that the entire family was reeling from the upheaval of the move from small town Plainville to a big city. Mom's return to work at the same time impacted everyone because we didn't know how to cope with the drastic changes.

Dad, who was still adjusting to his new role as a dental professor, suddenly found himself thrust into another new role of overseeing the household chores. Mom often worked weekends, too. Once she returned to work, she resigned from most household tasks. That certainly messed with Dad's head about the "traditional" role men held in the home at that time. No one was happy.

She now understands that they were all just doing the best they could. She feels how they *are* all very grateful that she was born and that she is an important part of the family.

 Little Glenda is finally free from all of the locked up hurt and sadness. Now a welcome part of the whole me, she is lonely no more.

Present Day

I am filled with gratitude for every experience I've shared with my family, even the awful ones. I believe that the unconditional love with which we helped Mom birth herself to the other side, brought healing to her soul and mine.

As Grandmother told me during my counseling session with Val, we healed our female ancestral line, too. Now when I think of them, I feel a deep peace that was never before present. All that remains is the Love which carried us through our experiences in Mom's final days.

We had a beautiful memorial service for Mom the August after she passed. I still have her ashes. On a sunny afternoon a few weeks later, the three of us went to the church memorial garden where

Dad's ashes are buried. We gathered some of the dirt from under the bush where they lay and combined it with Mom's ashes. It's time to scatter them to the winds.

May they fly high and free!

ACKNOWLEDGMENTS

$\mathscr{S}$ometimes we never know the impact we have on those whose lives we touch. The people mentioned here helped me climb out of a deep depression caused by my medical condition. Without their support, I never would have put these words to the page.

Thank you for showing up in my life. Your gentle, compassionate encouragement coaxed me back into a rich and fulfilling life. With your help, I found the strength and deep will to reach for all of the goodness life offers.

To Dawson Church, Ph.D., Director of EFT Universe. You are more than just my mentor. Your guiding light fueled Nothing Left but Love into existence. I gratefully call you, "friend."

To my friend Marilyn McWilliams, a dedicated EFT practitioner who selflessly volunteers her time helping Veterans with military-related PTSD. You gently guided my husband back from the life-threatening darkness he inherited in the Vietnam War.

To my good friends Vicki Carr and Susan Madden. Your much-appreciated, emotional support and mad editing skills rescued this book from the dusty shelf upon which it resided in my mind.

To my husband, my partner, my friend. How can I possibly thank you enough for coming into my life that hot July day so many years ago. Thank you for your support and technical help with this book. My dear, our years together seem just a moment in time. I believe the best is yet to come!

Lastly, I want to mention the people who helped us through Mom's death walk. To the Legacy Hospice Team of McMinnville, Oregon. You are the glue by which we held ourselves together in the dark, wee hours of those last mornings.

RESOURCES

I've included this list of books and other resources that I found extremely helpful. The beacons of hope I've listed provide valuable assistance in unwrapping the hidden healing potential inherent in the life and death journey.

Section 1: For Inspiration through the End of Life Process

Alexander, MED, Eben, *Proof of Heaven: A Neurosurgeon's Journey Into the Afterlife*. New York, NY. Simon & Schuster 2012.

Jenkinson, Stephen. *Die Wise: A Manifesto for Sanity and Soul*. Berkeley, CA. North Atlantic Books 2015.

Kübler-Ross, M.D, Elisabeth. *The Tunnel and The Light: Essential Insights on Living and Dying*. New York, NY: Marlowe & Company 1999.

Kessler, David. *Visions, Trips and Crowded Rooms: Who and What You See Before You Die*. Carlsbad, CA: Hay House, Inc. 2011

Roberts, Barbara K . *Death Without Denial, Grief Without Apology: A Guide for facing Death and Loss*. Troutdale, OR. NewSage Press 2002

Death Talk Project

One of the best new sources of help and support is provided through the Death Talk Project, formerly known as Death OK. Follow this link to their Facebook page
http://deathtalkproject.com/about/deathok/deathok-presenters/

Hospice Care

Your local medical team will have the information needed to connect you with a Hospice care provider in your area. I cannot sing their praises enough. They continue to offer grief support for a full year after your loved one departs.

Section 2: For Grief Assistance after the Loss of a Loved One

Grubbs, Geri. *Bereavement Dreaming and the Individuating Soul.* Berwick, ME.

Nicolas-Hays, Inc. 2004 www.nicolashays.com

I've also included a link to my sister Sherry's webpage. She is a certified practitioner specializing in grief work. These techniques were fundamental in rekindling her joy after the death of her son when he was only two and the subsequent early loss of her husband.

Sherry Rueger Banaka

Certified EFT Practitioner specializing in Grief Healing Work

Hillsboro, Oregon

Sherryruegerbanaka.com

sherryruegerbanaka@gmail.com

Section 3: For Assistance with your Personal Growth Work

I was open to the Love and Grace of my mom's end of life journey because of my willingness to face and heal my emotional wounds. I believe that the contrast of the hard times provides the background through which we experience the greatest joy, if we know how to glean the gifts.

Our mainstream, western culture is just now beginning to recognize the importance of learning about our emotional health. Healthy, happy people create happy, healthy environments. In my opinion, Energy Practitioners are a big part of healing the world one heart at a time.

Below, please find the links to the various organizations and techniques that have helped me the most with my own healing process. There is more information about these organizations on their websites. The EFT websites contain links to certified practitioners in your area. You will also find links to the many peer reviewed clinical trials, which are lending scientific credibility to the results I've achieved using these techniques.

My exploration into personal growth and healing began in the human potential movement of the early 80's. In the 90's a close friend of mine introduced me to an amazing woman known as Byron Katie. She was just beginning to launch on the scene with her simple, yet very powerful formula for finding real happiness and internal peace, regardless of life situation.

Today, her work spans the globe in its popularity. The Work consists of four simple questions to ask yourself when you are upset about a person or situation. Then you apply her technique called, "The Turnaround." Check out her website for the full story.

The Work of Byron Katie

As described on their website, "The Work is a way to identify and question the thoughts that cause all your suffering. Everything you need in order to do The Work is available free on this website." **Byronkatie.com**

Section 4: Energy Psychology Organizations

As mentioned in the Epilogue, Emotional Freedom Technique, (aka EFT or tapping) works by using the same energy pathways found in Chinese Acupuncture.

Tapping on the points while focusing on upsetting situations and feelings tells the body that the stress is not truly life threatening. The amygdala, the part of our brain hardwired for survival, calms down. The stress hormones decrease and the feel good hormones increase. For complete information, case studies, and a list of certified practitioners in your area, consult these organizations.

EFT Universe
Dawson Church, Ph. D
Director
EFTUniverse.com

Dawson is the author of a book called, *Genie in Your Genes.* (Energy Psychology Press; 2nd edition April 5, 2009).

This book was my first glimmer of hope that I could recover from my condition. Many of the documented clinical trials are covered in his book.

General Inquiries for the EFT Universe website:
Attention: EFT Support
1490 Mark West Springs Rd.
Santa Rosa, CA 95404
support@EFTuniverse.com

Follow this direct link to the research documentation. http://www.eftuniverse.com/scientific-research

The Tapping Solution, LLC
Nick Ortner, CEO and Author
TheTappingSolution.com
Host of the annual Tapping World Summit, a free online event held each spring.

EFT Catalyst
Certified EFT Practitioner Marilyn McWilliams
Based in Portland, OR. She currently offers free EFT for veterans dealing with chronic pain and stress in person and via the Internet. Her contact information is listed on her website. eftcatalyst.com

Energy Medicine by Donna Eden
http://innersource.net/em/about/donna-eden.html
As described on her website, Energy Medicine awakens energies that bring resilience, joy, and enthusiasm to your life – and greater vitality to your body, mind, and spirit! Balancing your energies

balances your body's chemistry, regulates your hormones, helps you feel better, and helps you think better. It has been called the self-care and development path of the future, but it empowers you NOW to adapt to the challenges of the 21st century and to thrive within them.

Section 5: For expert help with recovery from sexual trauma

Alina Frank, Master EFT Trainer

Providing Results Oriented Coaching since 2005

Best selling author of *How to Want Sex Again: Rekindling Passion Using EFT.* Difference Press. Washingtong, D.C. 2015.

Co-director of <u>EFT MBA,</u> Marketing & Business Academy for EFT Coaches

Finally, the support of your local spiritual center, church, or support group community can prove invaluable. It's important to know that we are never alone.

ABOUT THE AUTHOR

Glenda Rueger Payne is passionate about personal healing and spiritual growth and has dedicated her life to these studies.

She is an intuitive visionary who enjoys helping her clients unlock the hidden secrets of their inner world for personal growth and healing. She loves assisting others in finding their own path to personal fulfillment.

A resident of Oregon Wine Country, she enjoys family life with her husband and four cats. Her sisters remain a big part of her life.

CPSIA information can be obtained
at www.ICGtesting.com
Printed in the USA
LVHW041923310323
743128LV00001B/45